TIME WAS AWAY

ALAN ROSS AND
JOHN MINTON

TIME WAS AWAY

A Journey through Corsica

faber and faber

This edition first published in 2010
by Faber and Faber Ltd
Bloomsbury House, 74–77 Great Russell Street
London WC1B 3DA

Printed by Books on Demand GmbH, Norderstedt

A CIP record for this book is available from the British Library

ISBN 978–0–571–26992–1

To Roy and Kate Fuller,
again

INTRODUCTION

In 1947, when John Minton and I went to Corsica, the island was still more or less sunk in a post-malarial torpor, a situation common to its nearest neighbour, Sardinia. We were struck equally by the island's spectacular beauty and its listlessness, its young men unemployed and longing to emigrate. Such activity as there was had to do with politics or smuggling.

Now all that has changed. The flyblown villages of the interior that once offered nothing to visitors boast clean rooms and reasonable restaurants, the sluggish coastal towns have blossomed into thriving resorts, with five-star hotels and settlements reserved for *naturistes*. With improvements in health and the economy, and only the occasional bomb or demonstration in the cause of independence, the Corsica of the 1980s bears little resemblance to the island we travelled through.

In this sense *Time Was Away* is even more of a period piece than it might otherwise have been. But if the feel of the place is different, its nature and its landscape remain essentially unchanged. This is what John Minton drew and I tried to describe. For my part — perhaps over-influenced by the travel books of Graham Green and the detached, camera-eye style of Christopher Isherwood — I think I over-emphasised the island's seediness and faint air of menace. I was determined to let the place speak for itself, with no intrusive 'I' or 'We', a technique that I would not use again. However, if I have reservations about my own contribution to the book, I have none about John Minton's. His drawings, done so quickly and vividly on the spot, are among the most perceptive illustrations of that neo-romantic era.

Alan Ross
1988

A MAP OF CORSICA

For JOHN MINTON

AT FIRST the coasts and hills are only lines,
with boundaries marked in red, and sea
like muslin draped in blue around the edges;
the peaks are feathered in as if with mines.
Towards the East the signs are sparse, towns
clustered round the North and West, with only
daubs to blot the marshes in the swampy downs.

Engraved in colours round the map's pale sea
the symbols of the past are twined or hung
like standards onto charts and legends clung
with vines, in which a key to roads and history
is perched—while on the top the bald Napoleon
surveys Pasquale Paoli, an unwilling aide,
emerging from a book, a gown, and shining braid.

Lower down the natural means of life are laid,
wine in green glasses, grapes, and silver fishes;
clay pipes like targets stick from olive vases,
and corals glow with sunsets in pale dishes.
Amongst crustaceans spiked with salmon—but
undismayed—moufflon point their horns
at Bonifacio, and wear the sea like crowns of thorns.

The map will come alive; the towns grow dark
with olive, straight nosed faces, and south
the sandy bays be filled with keels of boats
and sails that enter in at dawn the mouth
that feeds them and is home. The marshes
now are fever, hills steep climbs, and overhead
the sky deep copper with the heat, but still not harsh.

"Time was away and somewhere else.
The waiter did not come, the clock
Forgot them, and the radio waltz
Came out like water from a rock:
Time was away and somewhere else."

Louis MacNeice

"Corsica had from the ancient Greeks the
name of Callista, on account of its beauty."

Boswell, *An Account of Corsica*

CONTENTS

PASSAGE

THE PORTUGAL lay alongside her jetty, smoke pouring from her yellow funnel; tugs sidled up and lay off her, waiting like confidence men. On her decks men sat in patches of shade, fanning off the flies.

Behind great wooden barriers on the quay, the crowd of passengers sweltered in an old warehouse building waiting to go on board. The ship was due to sail at four o'clock.

At four-fifteen the barriers were pushed ajar and in single file the crowd was allowed to cross over the rope at the foot of the gangway. Regularly every ten minutes a voice in French came through a microphone begging those at the back of the scrum not to push those in front. "There is plenty of time," the voice kept on repeating, "plenty of time", and from the depths of the sweating, anxious mass of people came answering, ironic comments, and hysterical gesticulations.

In reply to questions, a lounging official monotonously and disinterestedly repeated "She sails at four," right up till the last minute when at five-thirty the barriers were closed and most of the passengers were on board. A few stragglers, a weeping young half-caste brandishing a useless ticket, and a handful of waving girls and old women watched the backsprings cast off, the tugs nudge away in the stern, and the ship's head slowly edge out into the stream. The look in the half-caste's eyes was built up by an age of accumulated suffering, resentment and acceptance. "Somehow," the look said, "this rusty, overloaded steamer, with officers in white gazing down at the herd of people clustered on the for'ard decks, is a passport to new chances, to liberty, dreams, sun; somehow I am being cheated of it again. Last time I got to the port, this time to the barrier; and now it must begin all over again."

On board were cabins for three classes of passengers; the fourth staked claims to square feet of deck and tarpaulin, spread out rugs, baskets of food and wine, and prepared for a night out in the open. On the upper decks, in the bars and lounges, brightly dressed women sat about smoking, mostly the wives of business men on their way out for transactions in Tunis or Ajaccio, or the families of officials domiciled in Corsica.

But the for'ard deck was crammed with peasants returning from France, with young Corsican men who were coming home for their annual holiday or from their military service, with the hundred and one types of people who through choice or necessity found their living in Paris or Bordeaux or Marseilles—as engineers, clerks, postmen—and who found it preferable to staying in and living through the ennui of their own island.

The faces were of no uniform type—some were obviously enough peasants, old women with faces like paintings, lined and puffy, their bodies mountainous and immovable; the men darkish and wiry, short and with undistinguished features. But the girls were mostly blonde or red-haired, married in France and now going back to their husbands' homes; or else married to negroes, and on their way to Tunis, little half-caste children sticking to them and gazing about with huge brown eyes at the land disappearing in the ship's wake, the bread and sausage being spread out amongst the wine bottles and peaches, and the tangible world slipping away from them.

By sunset the French coast had sunk like a piece of dark ice behind the rim of the horizon. The bows of the ship pushed away water of a deep ink-blue, creased like tissue paper, and soon a moon drew a silver flare path across the course of the ship, cutting it diagonally. A few stars lay reflected on the sea like flowers printed out of chromium.

16

The wine and bread were packed up, and amongst the smell of peaches, stale sweat and garlic, a boy struck up on an accordion and girls danced together to ancient nostalgic dance tunes and the men leant against the ship's rail smoking.

On the deck above, the glasses clinked in the bar, and a gramophone played while couples danced in the coloured light like fireflies and sailors lay on coils of rope. To them it was the same as any day. But, below they were going home.

    .   .   .   .   .

The night grew cooler, the bodies on deck muffled like mummies. The masts tilted gently against the stars. The sleeping figures curled into one another in dumb embraces, the noise of the engines growing into their dreams and the salt touch of the sea air fanning their faces.

A few miles north, the Jewish immigrant ships were anchored while British naval escorts cruised up and down waiting for orders. The faint flash of an Aldis lamp flickered out a message against the horizon and from the other side an answer stuttered back. Then the masthead lights came closer together like magnets and moved away northward towards Marseilles with their unwilling cargo.

But on the *Portugal* there were no right or wrongs, no ethical conflicts in the situation. Life was what Fate ordained, a matter perhaps for approval or for complaint, but fundamentally only for acceptance. The world of great power units was a myth whose symbolism was already exploded; its rhetoric created only mistrust and indifference.

Amidships two nuns emerged out of their cabins and stood leaning out over the rail. Two Sisters from Ajaccio returning home? Perhaps two novices going out from France for the first time?

The nuns' faces were washed in the lemon flare of the moon, the lines rubbed out into pale, earnest shapes as their heads moved slightly and their voices floated and died against the wind's curve.

What really happened in the hearts hidden under those black flowing robes, the bodies crucified of beauty, the personalities robbed? Somewhere, did Faith still exist, unperverted by deception, by war, or human inadequacy?

The two shapes adjusted their hoods, arms emerging like cool flowers from the ice of their bodies. Then the folds buried their fingers again and the wind seemed warmer and human. The ship creaked in a slight swell, and on the fo'c'sle the store of bodies rolled against one another, like articles in a cheap box. A pig in a stained basket squeaked unceasingly, like a bad concertina.

    .   .   .   .   .

As it grew light Cape di Ferro became just visible, lightly pencilled in beneath the hesitant masonry of the clouds. The sea had grown flat calm—green, blue and purple in patches.

Like a porpoise shaking itself, the whole deck had suddenly risen out of its sleep, gabbling and shrieking in dialect French and Italian. Blankets were rolled up and stowed away; in a few minutes the old women dressed in their black mourning were reseated on their suitcases, their brood of children round them, all dressed ready and expectant, though the ship could not possibly get in for another three hours. Wine was produced, and loaves; the chatter began all over again. It might have been some group of pilgrims coming to new shores, hopefully restarting their history.

The land's contours increased, a magic-lantern slide coming into focus and showing huge purple mountains rising sheer from the water, lined and wrinkled like a lion's muzzle. At the base of the coastline odd scattered rocks, half-submerged, stretched out scaly and harsh into the shape of a crocodile. The young girls and men hung over the rails; the ship's gramophone was put on and Ajaccio came into sight round a sharp bend in the coast, first of all a lighthouse on Sanguinares and then the cemetery and garrison, white stone buildings under a sun already hot, with the green, scurfy hills sloping backwards behind the town.

The *Portugal* turned into the harbour shortly after seven, the gramophone playing "The More I See You" and on the quay a craning, gesticulating crowd like black insects surrounded by fishing boats and nets. A fast motor-boat circled the ship interminably, showing off its paces. At the main jetty the *Ville d'Ajaccio*, a black, one-funnelled steamer with paint peeling, was already in.

.　　　.　　　.　　　.　　　.

Ajaccio hangs down from the mountains like a suspended swimmer, arms outstretched that form the main waterfront, the back slightly humped down whose spine the main street runs north and south. Approaching from the sea the faded yellow façade of the front is broken only by the single white parting of the main road. For the rest the houses are tall, shuttered, and of an indifferently painted cream and orange plaster. A thin road covered in ruts is flanked by cafés, a few shops, and market stalls.

Hardly had the ship come alongside—with much fussiness and business of all sorts—than the peasants began lowering all their belongings on tough white ropes to relatives waiting on the quay below.

18

AJACCIO—THE TOWN FROM THE QUAY

A few cars were already drawn up, converted from lorries, and a number of donkey-drawn carriages with coloured sunshades.

The pigs, rabbits and dogs were lowered down in their boxes; parcels of less value were hurled regardlessly down onto the quay; and when the gangways were lowered a throng was waiting to descend, already rid of its luggage.

All the while, the voice of Tino Rossi crooned out its silky notes, the negroes and half-castes hung about irresolutely on the far rail and the sweat on the porters' backs and faces shone like some iced apéritif. By the harbour wall a man in a straw hat sprayed his donkey with a hose pipe, cursing when it shook its back, and afterwards embracing it.

The human cargo unloaded itself and rushed into waiting arms. On the bridge the immaculate Portuguese officers smoked cigarettes and took no part in the proceedings. Later in the day they sailed for Tunis.

Last off the boat, the nuns, in groups like pigeons, stood waiting till everybody had gone. They might indeed have been waiting for the Resurrection. Silhouetted against the blue-green sea, their white caps fluttering in sails, they looked remote and helplessly beautiful.

BONAPARTE'S legacy to Corsica was a hideous tombstone, a statue of himself on horseback surrounded by his four brothers, and a note in his Memoirs that most of all on Elba he missed the warm scent of the *maquis* on the hills above Ajaccio. Beyond that his voluntary part in Corsican life was negligible. He possessed a sense of family but not of what he considered minor responsibilities. Corsica was too small for his dreams, a prison he could only hallow by escape.

He remains only as a commercial proposition, his name appearing on innumerable shops of souvenirs, bakeries, streets—all the cafés are called Bar au 1ᵉʳ Consul, Napoléon's Bar, or Bar Buonaparte.

Some of them have already been superseded by Rue Foch, Foch's Bar, and in turn are being rapidly changed to Place de Gaulle, and so on —for respect is dependent on commercial and political fashion.

The streets were fairly full, the boat's arrival being a bi-weekly incentive to activity, that is to say a certain speculation, as opposed to physical labour. The market stalls were all up, the booths filled with melons, peaches, grapes, tomatoes, aubergines. The scents mingled and spread across the streets in heavy woven nets of perfume. Behind the booths women, mostly in black, sat on wooden boxes, legs apart, spitting out grape-pips. A child sat on a pavement, blood spouting from its knee which had been cut open till the flesh was like the inside of a ripe peach. Round about dogs lay on their backs in patches of shade and thin cats padded about on dancers' feet.

All up the main street the bars were open, their orange and blue awnings up, scattered handfuls of men sitting about talking, occasionally waving their hands wildly and then subsiding. Opposite the hotel in the main street, the white courtyard of the Préfeture was empty except for a blue-shirted attendant, sitting in an open office, wiping away the sweat, and swatting flies.

The Préfet is the nominal head of the Corsican Government, a nominee of France for a hardly considered Colonial fag-end. A General commands the garrison troops of the island, and an Admiral the naval base, but both are undeveloped, isolated, and not really of the island. The officials carry out their term of office, hurry back

21

to France, and pray the administration is not too closely inquired into.

But the politics which are the town's life-blood have nothing to do with France or the outside world. They are as individual as the prayers of the nuns. Signs are written up on the walls "*Vive de Gaulle*" or "*Votez Communiste*", but they have no relation to the symbols for which those names stand.

The politics are bound up with local personalities, themselves only emblems for various sides of commerce, intrigue, or the Black Market. De Gaulle has perhaps the greatest following, though the Mayor is a Communist. But soon there will be a new election, perhaps a new Mayor. Last time 30,000 shots were fired off on election day—not always at people, but simply as affirmations of an individual right. The hopeless, theatrical, romantic gesture, that has no relation to right or wrong.

But whoever gets in it will not affect the Government, except perhaps the cocaine will get into different hands, the oil be smuggled out by a different route, a new group of people have motor cars.

The talk in the bars goes on, the prices are quoted for sugar, oil, fish in Marseilles—these things which are native to the island and necessary are too valuable to be used. They fetch huge prices on the Côte d'Azur, are exchanged for drugs, for shoddy finery, for money to spend. But not for possessions or for organised living. History has taught loss. Too often everything has been swept away; to risk working for another man to reap the reward is not worth the effort.

So the natural industries are neglected, the mineral wealth never exploited. There is no labour for it and no incentive. The young men live by fishing or through their vineyards, but mostly they leave home. Home is only to return to, to remember in loneliness like Napoleon. There have been already too many local heroes for them to bear.

At midday the streets are empty, the market stalls closed up. The buses, blue and dirty yellow, wait round the Place de Gaulle till someone can be found to go in them. Under palm trees men lie stretched out on the benches in the Cours Napoléon.

Everybody rests, waits, watches. The air holds a mixture of indolence and hidden tension. Perhaps suddenly someone will drop a match, or stub out a cigarette and everything will begin. They will know by the signal that what is to be done must be done. The sleeping figures will come alive out of their wax, the hidden revolvers glisten in the copper light.

But the sign will never now be given, the Revolution never come. Only the talk, the strange looks, the listless waiting for nothing will continue. It is a cynical acceptance of the spirit, a resignation like the heat.

.   .   .   .   .

From the shoulders of the town, small streets run off in vertebrae down to the sea. Narrow, only a few feet wide, tall tenement houses rise up six and seven storeys on either side of the cobbled street. From window to window, banners under the sky, clothes hang up drying on coarse lines. The doorways are open except for curtains of raffia and bead. The gutters are splashed with refuse, over-ripe fruit, ordure. The smell of drains mingles with the scent of flowers and fruit, is washed away by momentary sea breezes, and returns to fall like a disease over the area. Flies move remorselessly in squadrons over the gutter.

On a high wall, above the name of the street, hangs the last reminder of the occupation—a tin placard pinned up—"OFF LIMITS TO ALLIED TROOPS". Nobody has bothered to move it. What would be the use, they say, when one day it will be put up again, perhaps in a different language ?

The successive, unceasing occupations have left their mark on the faces of people, on their habits, character, institutions; in remnants of cruelty, oppression, endurance, impermanence. Greeks, Carthaginians, Tuscans, Genoese, French, Spanish, British, Germans, Italians— what natural character could be left unsucked by this leeching, year after year, generation after generation ?

Only great men could have retained and kept a soul alive and integrated—but the great Corsicans, like the best produce, have always been for export. Or they have died, broken by stronger powers, in alien soil, like Paoli, the name of a street, or a Café Bar, their substitute for a Constitution, for peace or prosperity, or a grave in the cypress-lined cemetery, west of Ajaccio, with its vaults over each tomb like temples, or mausoleums, or lavatories.

At night, windows are lit in the high-up, tenement houses—each room has become a stage-set, isolated and complete in itself. Shadows move across the walls or ruffle the bead curtains; faces stare out from the darkness of unlit windows down into the street. At what ? With what dream, or hope or ambition shut away like a pressed flower forgotten in the pages of an unread book ? Perhaps there was no dream, no hope from the start—except the waiting for what was never known to happen, or the sudden pulsation of a face seen under a lamp,

24

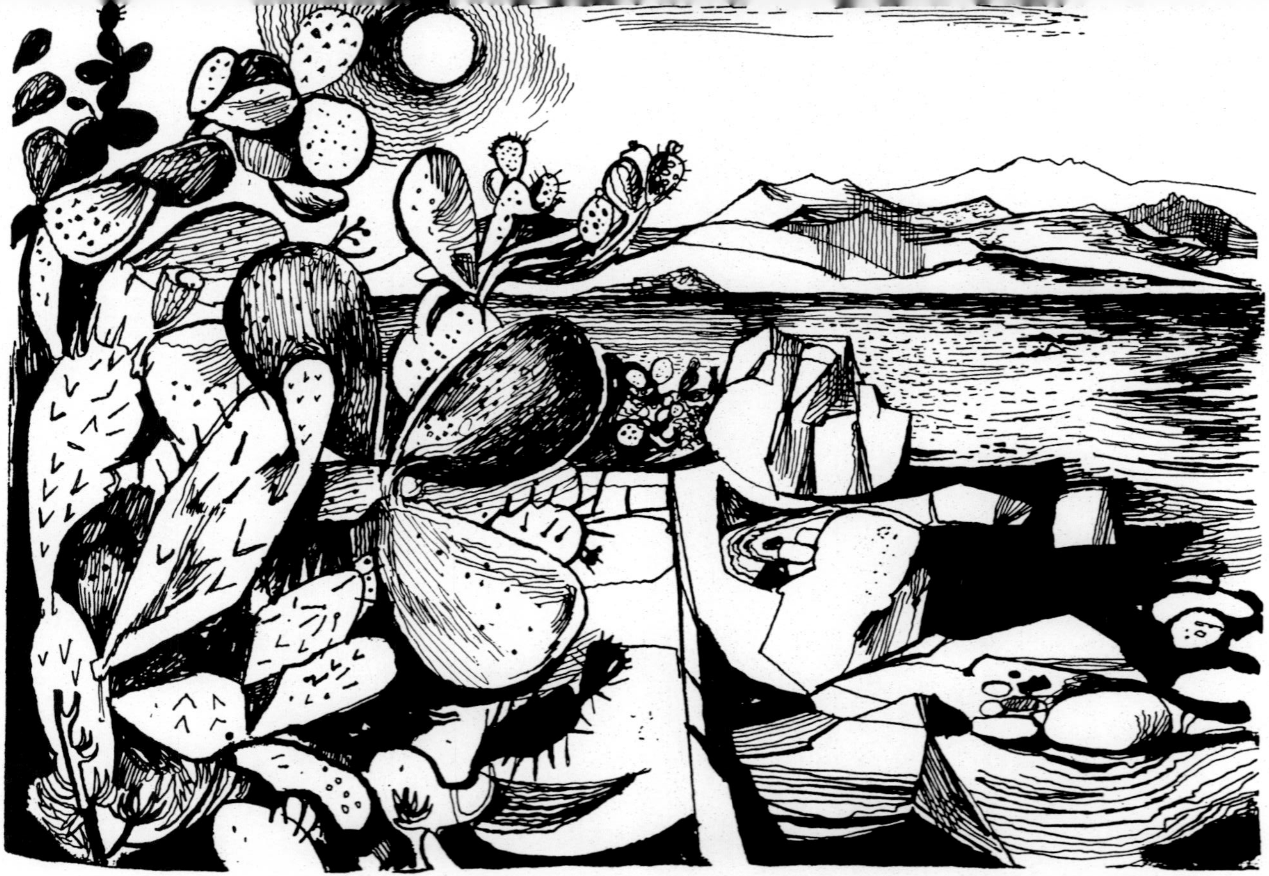

AJACCIO—CACTUS AND SEA

a gun pointed and fired and a man dead in a gutter licked into death by pariahs. The smell only, the pity, the distant badly-played music hang like a permanent motif over the rooms framed with faces and tilted oil paintings. The fruit lies heavy on the window boxes; a girl plays over and over again the same bars of music, and breaks down each time at the same chord.

The streets run into each other like honeycombs, bars underground with arched beams, caves filled with barrels and the smell of alcohol. Garlic and fruit dress them in their frames of orange light. A few girls sit desultorily at tables, legs crossed under short cotton frocks, flowers or ribbons stuck loosely into their hair. But mostly the bars are empty, the proprietor sunk over a table in his shirtsleeves or fanning himself with a paper.

Outside on the pavements whole families sit motionless, staring into space, silent; the children lie asleep on their mothers' laps and cats slink up and down like pimps or detectives. It is too hot to sleep, there is nothing to talk about.

.   .   .   .   .

Napoleon's mother gave a name to a cinema, besides her son's birth in the Rue St. Charles. It is apposite enough as a symbol of the historical sense that has been corrupted under oppression and its counterfoil of commercialism.

The great Corsicans, like Paoli, fought for History, for the striking out of new roads on the map whose rights of entry were not dependent on foreign interests. But they were always beaten back or sold up in their absence. The historical sense was destroyed till it became no more than a bait on a picture postcard.

"Yes," the picture postcard says, and the cinema, the dance hall, the Bar au 1ᵉʳ Consul. "Corsica has produced great men, patriots, heroes against oppression, emperors. Blood of all nations has flowed into our landscape peopling it like rivers. But must there be only history, the past, the shadow of great events lying over us?"

The coin is two-sided: on the other side is the ship carrying stores to Tunis, the two-piece bathing costumes, the silk stockings, the coloured shirt, the American Bar. And under the counter of morality the drugs, the absinthe, the girls in Marseilles.

Nothing, they say, is any longer important; the great days, the past and the future are terms without meaning—like forms, regulations, the garrison soldiers. They exist, but in the dream world of drugs they have no meaning like the illusions of the senses, the far-away

26

AJACCIO—STREET AT NIGHT

frontier where the false and the real merge like lovers into each other's arms.

Death alone is permanent in life—death, the sea and the tall hills. The rest is an endurance, heat, disease, labour which come like visitations or stay always as part of the scenery. But in dreams there is the escape, the new world, the fulfilment, which if they fail or are defeated, compensates them for the endless, eternal waiting. Afterwards the world grows real again, a landscape of cactus, blue sea, flowers, poverty and tuberculosis.

The means of life are sufficient, so there is no need for effort. What is necessary is done early, the rest is put off, unpunctual as old bus time tables, or done without trouble. The virility is exported, the cleverness that remains is the art of the wide boy, the pimp, the beachcomber, where money comes easily behind the hand and the price is the price of a fast car, a gramophone, or a visit to the pictures.

Beauty remains as the natural justification, but it is a beauty that is built for the stranger; the home world stops short at the quay, the scenery grows too familiar, the steamer is only a letter whose contents are money.

.   .   .   .   .

Twice a week the boats come in from Bone on their way to Marseilles. For a few hours they accomplish what the Revolution cannot—they galvanise everybody into activity, the quay becomes charged with excitement. Porters carry off loads of luggage into the hotels and the Bars simmer with expectancy.

Nothing is going to happen, but the sense of movement, of contact with the outside world is restored. The life-blood of new people for a few hours rejuvenates and recreates a sense of purpose.

From the hotel window the ship is like a scene from an expensive film; the dark shadows of the hills rise out of the water in the background, the navigational light flicks out incessantly—dash, dash, dot, dash—from the jetty, and in the foreground the ship itself—a theatre built on water—throws into relief the brief focus of lives that are suspended for a moment, anonymous cyphers who move from one place to another giving and withdrawing vitality from whatever they touch and leave.

The palm trees are lit up on the quay, the barren water-front is become an unreal garden. Behind, the green crème-de-menthe light of the seaplane base remains constant, and far up on the hill the dying fires of the burnt out *maquis* glimmer in hopeless beacons.

28

The donkey traps shake out their bells, loaded with luggage. In the Café du Golfe, *Madame* struggles with her figures in a stream of arrivals. A French barrister and his blonde Corsican wife sit talking of their home in Paris with a First Empire charm, their daughter discussing Baudelaire and drawing fashion plates of Josephine on the crinkled table cloth.

The boat leaves punctually at midnight, two hours late. The curtains are drawn again, the chatter subsides. The watchers return to their vigils.

THE ROAD SOUTH

THE BUS for Porto Vecchio leaves every day at eight from the Café Ajaccio. By then the sun is burning hot, the bus itself—a Rapide Bleu—is washed down with water and the passengers are waiting in the café. At ten to eight the driver starts loading the luggage up on top of the roof; suitcases, blankets, prams, baskets, tin trunks all lashed down together. Then at eight he makes the roll call of ticket holders and one by one everybody gets in, clasping bottles of wine, bags of peaches and grapes—a few soldiers going home, farmers, peasants with guns, women in black with simple mapless faces, young girls lipsticked but clumsily inelegant.

The pantechnicon sets off, its cargo travellers in search of a new land, behind them the images of the night steamer, the chromium bar, the café-dancing—in front the home, the forgotten loyalty, the shackles of an evaded responsibility.

The road follows the curve of the bay, up by the landing signals of the air base and begins to climb steadily through a belt of orchards, vegetable gardens and farmland. In a few minutes Ajaccio is a small, unreal model, the sea blistered with the light of the sun, and the white landing stages burning like powder.

Three priests enter the bus, two in black cassocks and one in white who is a Dominican from the settlement in Corbara near Calvi on the north-west coast. He speaks a little English and explains that though everybody in the island is baptised it makes no difference to their irreligiousness; they come and go, do what they please and take no trouble to improve themselves. The human desire for progress finds only barren soil in the island. Some of the people read, some write. The children are obliged to go to school, but none of the older people speak any language but Corsican and scarcely understand French. Nearly everyone is a Catholic, save for a few Jews and Protestants up in Bastia and Calvi. But as far as their activities are concerned, it is all the same thing. The young Dominican shakes his head sadly.

A man in the front of the bus reads the *Journal de la Corse*, his paper open at a page headed by a '*lettre ouvert à de Gaulle*'. Beside it are reports of outbreaks of anti-Semitism in Liverpool and Glasgow, windows of Jewish shop-owners being broken in vengeance for the

31

death of two British sergeants in Palestine. The Vendetta is unending. But not here, they say, where Paoli ruthlessly stopped the system of family vengeance as his first act in power. The local bandits in fact were rarely criminals in the dangerous sense but mostly refugees who feared a corrupt justice or the "framed" trials of interested Judges— men who often had committed no crime at all but were afraid of being victimised. So they lived like outlaws in the hills, were fed by friends and relatives, and though their whereabouts were well-known to every-one, the authorities dared not touch them.

The priests are asleep, drugged by the scent of the *maquis* which hangs like an anaesthetic, or by the heat. The road still rises, precarious as a scenic railway.

There is less cactus now, but alternate belts of olive, ilex and pine, interspersed with patches of desiccated scrub and grey rock, under whose shade donkeys lie stretched out. They scatter at the sound of the bus, their nervous, over-sensitive feet knocking loose stones onto the road.

At Cauro, the walls of a small village suddenly materialise out of the undergrowth, the sides of the houses draped with flags and scrawled with *Vive Giraud* and *Vive de Gaulle*. For even up here the political game is played, where the noise of a radio brings the voice of Tino Rossi, the local boy made good, soothing away the tales of power politics, betrayals, economic swindles as though they were so many stories in a book of legend. But, remorselessly, in time their effect is felt, and brought home to the faithless lonely pink houses isolated like toys, miles from any community, living only by shot-gun and barter. But every day the radios spill out poison, creating their false dreams and destroying the simplicity of acceptance.

A bus comes up from Bonifacio, and the bus drivers wave as they pass, turning off into the scrub to let each other through. Below, dried streams give out in despair, where amongst ravines blank with the polished faces of boulders, the sun grows merciless over the scrub which already smokes like the fires left by a decamping army.

A Corsican girl gets on the bus, having just flown over from Aix where she studies to be an English teacher. Her home is at Quenza where she comes back for holidays.

But not for long, she says. Her mother a Parisienne, her father a Corsican, she burns with a hysterical hatred and resentment of her nationality, and equally with a fervid worship for England, the door to all dreams.

"They are all lazy, the Corsicans," she cries out, "dirty, lazy, useless. They would rather take their sisters to Marseilles and trade them in the

THE MOUNTAIN ROAD TO PORTO VECCHIO

port for a few weeks so they can come home and loaf the rest of the year, than do a day's work."

Her bitterness is increased by the inferior social position of the woman in the Corsican household. Her mother had married in Paris, but now found out her mistake. "But I won't repeat it," she says, "I wouldn't marry a Corsican if it was the last thing I did."

All round the peasants, the young men, stare stupidly at this language they do not understand.

The road turns sharply south of Aullène and swings round above a green curled scalp of trees through which the lower road runs like a powdered parting.

Huge *cols* hang in a frieze of livid saffron and prune on the skyline, but already the landscape has become a drug, enormous and wonderful, but over-picturesque—there is nothing left for the imagination to fill in, so it becomes boring sooner or later, like an over-handsome, characterless man.

At intervals small settlements built into the rock, shacks covered with straw and filled with children, hens, refuse, emerge round a bend in the road and for a few yards along, tombstones, orange in the sunlight, mark the lost generations whose meaning never quite materialised but whose existence was sufficient. They had loved, hated, lost—like everything else that had a place in the only comprehension that existed, the comprehension of suffering. Strange mosque-like buildings materialise out of thin air, castles which do not seem really to exist and have no purpose, but which symbolise the fluttering tenuous flags of hope that made the future possible.

The deft threads of living, the roads, the sudden red flowers of the houses pulsing like wounds in the green heart of the hill, are delicate images that once broken, once destroyed, have no substitute—no new symbol can be ever quite so natural.

By Serra men appear bare-chested out of stone quarries, cigarettes dangling from their mouths, rivers of sweat running down from their necks. Their eyes follow the bus, which runs across their gaze like blood running into an artery. Escape, escape, the wheels say—and in the eyes of the lost, longing legion of men, desire for escape blots out the lust for the Woman. The aeroplane, the steamer, the bus—these are the objects of love, the vehicles of envy.

Round the walls of the few houses are chalked messages "Sporting Bar", "Dancing", "*Vive le 4ᵐᵉ Republique*"—but who drinks and who dances, who is not as everyday an object of life as a table, a brother, a sister?

Giant shrubs lean over the road and roots rear up in grotesque rubber gesticulations. From windows cut out of mud, black-dressed, timeless women stare out of their frieze of small, stone Virgin Marys, dance music, fern, and tombs.

The driver sends a jet of spittle accurately onto a signpost. The road zig-zags down to Zonza.

At Quenza the anglophile Corsican girl gets out, her chatter of Thackeray, film stars, and petty gentility sucked into the unprepossessing Hotel de Diamante. The bus stops for half an hour, and in a cool crude room with primitive drawings and dance music coming from Paris, black bread, sausage, wine, and cheese are brought by an unshaven peasant, a pistol half hanging out of an oily belt.

Soon the Dominican gets out, and climbs up a steep path to a white Mission on the hillside. From hidden mountain clearings, bearded revolutionary-looking peasants board the bus and again get off where no dwelling-house is visible to the eye.

Telegraph poles cut across the route, grey against the lolling boulders, and at Zonza the tall trees crowd on the roadsides in clusters like lanky, short-sighted schoolgirls. The bark is all cut away, leaving an even brown stocking for the trunk of the tree, and in huge waves, heavy as incense, the perfume of the undergrowth falls in a drug over the hillside.

Now and again trails of dust-filigree stretch in thin nets onto the lower reaches of the rough bramble, and after patches of boulder and rock, grapevines cling to the narrow walls on the ledge of the turnings.

The bay of Porto Vecchio, scissor-shaped, blue, swings like a mirror out of the distance and the mountain shadows drop in gaunt robes over the water.

PORTO VECCHIO

Hɪsᴛᴏʀʏ ran dry here, a Genoese stronghold built overlooking the bay almost cut off by hills. The whole port, the commanding position, the wide harbours promised enormous development, but somewhere the imagination gave out, with houses half finished, the railway petering into marshes, the projected jetties rotting like poisoned arms.

The effort of cultivation was arrested, a gesture frozen in mid-air, and over everything hung the deserted atmosphere of an abandoned town. The few people in the street sat about on dirty pavements as if under some terrible sentence. Everyone else had gone into the mountains, the only refuge from the swamps, the malaria, and the decay.

In a semi-circle round the town, collapsing battlements poised over the filthy green of the gulf and beyond them clumps of cork and olive trees reached high up into the mountains. But in the town the atmosphere of defeat had undermined the imagination. Rotten fruit lay about on the pavements.

Down by the sea wall a solitary sailing boat with a pale blue sail idled on the windless water. On the jetty naked fisherboys chased one another into the sea, and under water grappled continuously. From a few wooden shacks washing hung out, and silent women sat nursing their babies on their verandahs over the water.

The shore was littered with dead fish, their mouths bared in the look of soldiers come upon dead in a battlefield, and, round about, rusty steel hoops lay by huge piles of cork, stored like shell cases the whole length of the beach. Anchors, washed up boats, gutted hulls, and huge red buoys straddled the green saucer of sea, paraphernalia no longer wanted; a few yards into the water a charred chair and a rusty table sat waiting for an occupant, macabre and eternal.

From the marshes cicadas and frogs kept up an orchestra of noise that went on day and night. When a stone was lifted, lizards ran out into crumbling fields of timber that were strewn about, refugees with some terror on their conscience, like people whose gaze can never meet for fear of something being found out.

In white cases on the soft edge of the swamp salt lay stacked, tiny pyramids bright as chalk, like the blocks scattered round fields during war to prevent the landing of aeroplanes. The salt engine beat away in a pulse continuously—one felt if it stopped, life would stop too.

PORTO VECCHIO—LA PORTE GENOISE

THE LIGHTS came out in the narrow alleyways, the music of "Laura" drifted from a nasal gramophone, over and over again. The water moved apathetically in the bay below, a few eyes stared out of windows into the semi-darkness. In cave bars with names like Café des Beaux Arts, Café d'Istanbul, Bar Franco-Anglais, men in white vests played cards, the women and girls sitting about doing nothing, idly looking for some object for their gaze to seize on and then dropping their look, birds shot down in their flight. An American prophylactic sign hung up on a wall in the main street, a remnant of a short termed occupation and crude murals of semi-naked girls ran round the walls of the hotel dining-room, bad, but heavily expressive in the complacent portrayal of lust, a mixture of the postures of dancing girls in an Egyptian frieze and the blank, expressionless poses of film stars.

Dinner in the hotel was crayfish, pieces of dry meat, rough bitter wine, and melon—but inadequate, small portions, so that one was always hungry ; flies settled on the bread, and walked slowly round the rims of the plates and glasses.

The owner of the restaurant, small, grey-haired, plump, but with kindly, untroubled blue eyes, sat at a table on the road-front looking up emptily from the pale lakes of his gaze at the mountains. Up there was the world, the repose, the purity, the singing.

In the summer no work is done in the hills. Most of the people have saved enough from the salt, the cork, and the fishing to last out without need of any other occupation. "Up there," repeated the *patron*, "they rest, and make ballads."

The Corsicans rehearse death; their ballads, their laments, their poems are all embroideries of the circumstances of death and preparation for mourning. Their beauty is all in the abjectness of the regret, the abasement before and celebration of loss, a flutter of the hands in salute or forgiveness or grief. Then it is all over, the end of the responsibilities of birth. The circle has been completed.

Off the hill road a rough camp was constructed for German prisoners of war. They had been there since 1943, first Occupiers, then workers

40

on the roads, the only signs of activity in the streets during day. Stripped to the waist they chipped the white blocks of the stone at the roadside, their forage caps green against the rich brown of their bodies. They hardly spoke: their dreams, their emotions dropped slowly into the sponge of the marshes. They became absorbed without any trace or effect on their environment. From the shade of trees, the inhabitants watched them at work; two alien worlds side by side, unable to communicate, with nothing in common.

The lights from the German windows went out in the darkness, a hundred and fifty existences switched over to an inner world whose destroyed landscape they had never seen.

The cinema was shut up, peeling posters hanging from old hoardings. Only in winter did it function, sporadically bringing the faces of out-moded beauties, introducing a few new slang words and hair styles already out of date. The plot, the events were already passed by, more unreal than if they had been centuries old. But it didn't matter, for the curious, human contact it established had no relation to time.

After a few hours, the houses, the people, the smell seemed already familiar, as if life had only existed there and in no other surroundings. The mountains were an iron curtain behind which Ajaccio, the Continent, England were stages further and further back in time, but no longer existing. Letters, papers, magazines could be only messages made up in a game of make-believe, with no real urgency, no implications beyond their mere fact.

A wind began to get up, blowing clouds of dust in the main street, banging shutters in the balconied houses. The thin, lace mosquito curtains moved behind the iron bars of the windows—the ghosts of purdahed women imprisoned in the nervous twitching of the lace.

Upstairs, in the hotel, large moorish rooms with purple settees, coloured porphyry vases, and Louis Quatorze chairs adjoined stone unfurnished hovels in which children slept naked and dirty on mats, and old women sat doubled up in sleep or watchfulness by the windows. Thought must have run out years ago.

On the walls of the bedroom framed portraits of Bonaparte, Robespierre and Danton looked over at one another. The plans were all used up and only Time remained—Time, in which their deaths had already said all they had to say. In a bookcase by the bed were the *Fables of La Fontaine*, a *History of French Literature*, an Italian dictionary, novels by Victor Hugo and Georges Sand, a manual of elementary science. A pail of water stood by the window, and the moon lit up the old ramparts of the town, ghostly, remote façades outliving their functions like everything else here—the roads running out into overgrown paths, houses suddenly abandoned, barracks with gutted windows empty and forgotten.

All night long, the wind blew in warm against the curtains, and the harsh creaking from the river increased and died down in spasms.

BUS STOP

WAITING for the bus to Bonifacio—
which arrives between four-thirty and seven according to the heat and
number of passengers—there is nothing to do but sit out on the hotel
terrace and drink endless glasses of *pastis*.

Down the narrow street to the sea the cocks crow minute after minute,
answering each other like echoes. In the distance below them the salt
slabs stand out white as tents or ice against the cobalt sea. Everyone
is asleep still, a civilisation laid out by the debauchery of ennui.

.   .   .   .   .

But the bus was delayed for some obscure reason and did not
arrive at all. Instead, they said, it would arrive to-morrow. As a
sort of consolation a man drove round the streets in a car with a
loudspeaker announcing a film for the evening—the first one since
the heat.

The cinema was down past the hardware shop and the few stalls
called Au Paradis des Dames. By half-past nine a moderate crowd
had collected outside the box office, gesticulating and arguing about
tickets, and eventually allowing itself to be pushed inside.

The cinema was a small whitewashed building with crumbling walls
on which were displayed murals of American Military Police in an
Elysium of semi-naked girls and tropical islands.

The seating consisted of some twenty or thirty benches which
stretched across the width of the hall; half-way down the cinema was
a barrier dividing the reserved seats from the few benches in the front
where a milling claque of children were strewn about, shouting in ill-
co-ordinated unison "*Commencez! Commencez!*"

The film began about twenty minutes after time, owing to the late
arrival of the Communist Mayor and his family who occupied a row
of balcony seats alongside the projector. The programme began
with an educational film on Climate, the origin of tides and winds and
so on, accompanied by a sequence of charts on which self-propelled
lines moved about. Occasionally this was varied by actual photographs
of trees, clouds, and thunder with immensely dramatic background
music as if some great human tragedy was being played out.

Then came the news: Madame Peron, received by Bidault, grinning and kissing children, waving to vast crowds from a shining limousine, and recalling the pale effigies of Hitler and his flower-garlanded heroines; Mrs Roosevelt, receiving the posthumous Médaille Militaire of her husband; a Commemoration Service for members of the Dutch Underground murdered by the Nazis; a bicycle race, madly cheered by the audience, with a Corsican competitor who received special applause and came in fifth.

Finally, amidst jeers and encouragement, the big film began, Danielle Darrieux in *Une Fausse Maîtresse*. After great flickerings on the screen, upside down credits, and raucous background music, the opening shots appeared—a big circus tent, clowns practising, men on parallel bars, and a fiery-faced fluffy-haired girl refusing a cigarette and extracting a cigar from her top-pocket. At moments the sound disappeared and the characters became savage caricatures, mouthing and waving their hands in helpless uncommunicativeness.

Then the sound would come on and the screen melt into darkness, the action going on under a blanket of night, as if something too obscene had had to be blacked out. Across this a bewildering series of incidents was flashed, a football match, a scene in a barber's shop, a strip-tease on a trapeze and the inevitable undressing episode with brassières and knickers being thrown over a screen; and then Miss Darrieux appeared, pert and unruffled in a dressing-gown.

The wooden seats had grown unbearably hard, and a cross-talk of conversation had sprung up amongst the urchins, who became silent only when for a second or two the clowns reappeared in a circus scene, but the camera always left them after a few seconds and fastened onto the protagonists of the plot, three or four smart young men with well-trimmed moustaches and flashing teeth.

The action followed routine lines, moments of comedy, quarrels in the circus, the smartest of the young men trying to win Miss Darrieux by sending her flowers, driving her about in a carriage in Paris and entertaining her against a smooth background of white marble rooms, roses, and champagne bottles—all to no success.

But after a few setbacks, outraged innocence and face slappings, Miss Darrieux for some quite inexplicable reason seemed to find the rather oily young man acceptable after all, and as her lips joined his and the camera tilted up into their faces enlarging them and making them suddenly beautiful, chords of great black music welled up from behind their eyes and the letters F-I-N flashed onto the screen.

The sound petered out as the last few feet of film were run off, the solitary fan stopped circulating and the lights came on with the audience already mixed up in a scrum for the door.

Outside the stars were out, bringing the white houses into relief against the curving lines of the hillside. A few people were sitting staring at the edge of the road and the strange drugging scent of the trees hung over the air. The croaking was still coming up from the river below, a thousand little knitting needles clacking together.

FACES WITHOUT FUTURE

THE APATHY, the staring idleness of the children, the lack of ambition in the men is the result of centuries without economic conflict. The island is a well out of which the means of life can be drawn as required—wine, fruit, salt, birds, honey, fish. There is no need for any organisation in acquiring them, and beyond what is actually necessary for moderate living, there is no point in acquiring any more.

Possessions breed their own responsibilities and after having been bled of their material prosperity by one occupying power after the other, no one has the interest to start over again. So after doing his military service, and perhaps spending a year or so on the Continent to save up some money, the Corsican comes home and lives on whatever he can buy with his savings—a shop, an inn, a few acres of cultivated land. There is little industry and the land practically works itself, so freed from worry he has the rest of his life in front of him to exist, to play cards and to sleep. And so the young men of ambition leave home for good.

The proud, fiery, individual violence appears to have been drained from the national character, perhaps by cross-breeding, perhaps by the slump in energy after the abandonment of the lost cause of independence. The failure to achieve that is a sort of hump in the middle of Corsican history; after it everything flops back on to a listless plain.

All the specialised natural products—crayfish, olive oil, chestnuts, briar, timber, coupled with various drugs—are clumped together at Ajaccio or Bastia and shipped off by merchants for sale at high prices in the south of France, and the inland districts of the island are left with nothing. As a result, and to further the exportation of everything, the peasants inland live very simple, primitive lives, eating roughly and very little, drinking only a glass or so of coarse wine a day, and with no amenities of life—no drainage, no comforts, no normal imports to redress the balance of their exports. Instead, the money is saved and a few weeks' negotiation brings in enough to last the rest of the year.

Yet the lines of communication are there, and the faint infiltrations of urban life—Dubonnet advertisements stuck on peasants' cottages, Shell petrol signs, flashy café hoardings, photographs of film stars

46

SIMON AND JEAN PAUL

pasted onto walls—stick out like the first sores of a disease, whose origins and meaning are never quite understood.

.   .   .   .   .

The "typical" face rarely emerges; instead there are a great many different, watered-down varieties, not by any means all dark. In the hills here the men are fairly well built, but under medium height, and dwarfed by the German working parties. There is little fire left in the eyes; far more a sort of indifferent resignation, a placidity in the contours of the face as though a sponge had been drawn across it, wiping off any of the more dangerous harshnesses. The faces are rarely beautiful, the structure of the bone too loose, as if the strength of expression was supported only by some invisible prop which might at any moment collapse.

The children have a strange disturbing repose which varies from quietude to a look of animal stupidity. Occasionally when smiles switch up their gaze and their white teeth flash in knives of approval, they achieve a kind of naturalness and simplicity which later appears to grow out of them.

The women all look old before their time, dirty and untidy, living the life of servants. The young girls are either pallid and characterless or else incongruously slashed with make-up and gold teeth, their youth maturing quickly to coarseness.

In Ajaccio there were some startling faces amongst the girls, one in particular with pale delicate skin, grey-brown eyes under dark eyebrows and a wide forehead from which auburn hair was brushed down in long page-boy style. The face came towards a thin fragile chin. The eyes were full of a melancholy brooding which spoke of a hankering after a private world locked up and inaccessible because there was no key to fit it.

There, many of the girls were beautifully built, blonde with brown, good skins and dressed in smart, naturally-worn modern clothes. But in the faces of the darker girls there was a pinched look, destroying the harmony and creating an effect of slight distortion.

PORTO VECCHIO—JEAN VALIN

THE CEMETERY BY THE SEA

THE POSTAL bus service that left the next day was a faded blue lorry, with loose green canvas over the back that flapped about in armless sleeves. There was nothing to sit on but a few rough wooden crates that were being sent to Bonifacio and which jumped to the canvas roof each time the lorry went over a bump. The only other occupants were a wiry little peasant, his wife dressed in black, and their child, a pallid little boy with a round straw hat perched in a bowl on the top of his head. The mother and father were very Italian looking, a typical organ-grinder family transported out of an American film.

The road was wider than the normal mountain routes and went through a valley of cork trees, twisting away from the sea and following the shape of the coastal inlets.

A few miles out of Porto Vecchio, out of nothing but scrub and bare hillsides a shining white cemetery emerged, set back a few hundred yards from the road and glittering like a mirage. Each grave was lined with overhanging trees and at its head or by its side a small temple, rounded, with a turret, or square with pinnacles, stood sentinel in memory to some peasant killed in war. Then the scrub, the coarse, green-scratched hills began again.

Round a bend in the road a whole charred area loomed up black and naked, the bushes all burned to fine particles, gritty like pieces of coal dust. A fire must have caught the *maquis* near the top of a crest and swept down, burning the bridge over a ravine, and propelling itself up the other side of the hill. The air was vacant with the barren desolation of some human disaster, like an accident at a pit-head.

The bridge hung uselessly in shattered fingers of wood unable to hold themselves up and the road diverged into the scrub itself and rejoined the old route half-way up the hill.

Soon the stone buildings of the fort of Bonifacio were just visible, a confectionary pink in the evening sun.

BONIFACIO

BETWEEN Porto Vecchio and Bonifacio something changes in the atmosphere—as if a frontier had been passed, or the news of a battle received. A sense of life begins to grow again out of the landscape, a purposiveness which is not due to any marked physical change. The approaches to the town are the same criss-cross of hills, patchy scrub, and white partings up the mountains dropping down to fields of marsh—the same as mark the countryside all up the east coast.

But the air seemed suddenly sweet and purified coming to it in the evening, and a cool settled over the streets like a hand pressed over the temples.

The road turned suddenly, and at the bottom of the hills the blue water of the port lay glassy between the stuccoed plaster houses. The rusty hull of a sunk ship heaved itself out of the sea like some monster in agony.

The inlet, almost entirely cut off by the scissors of the hills, was lined with small sailing boats, rowing boats, and a few launches. The grey steamer *Iles Sanguinares* lay off a wooden jetty. Small, nearly-naked boys crawled about the boats. An Italian training ship, blown up by the Germans, lay on its side.

The houses at the water's edge were pale pink and blue, but mapped with filthy stains which were inlaid with dirt and green shutters. Old women peered through the windows and girls stood about in the dark doorways.

Stone steps led up a steep incline to the fort and the cluster of houses which lay at the top hung precariously over the leaning rock. A slight push of nature and the whole thing would have collapsed into the sea.

Up and down the steps people led donkeys loaded with bags, animals little bigger than dogs. At the top the cobbled path swung up round a hairpin bend, into a tunnel fluttering with bats and out into the town itself—a labyrinth of small, dark streets with lights burning inside rooms like caves, barrels heaped on the floor near the walls.

Further up chestnut trees uncurled, green and fawn tasselled, out of the bare stone, sudden flowerings of compassion amongst the dark alleyways running down in all directions, meeting and recoiling in

51

confusion, being driven back into the wide compound of the citadel at the top.

The barracks formed a square of long sand-coloured buildings, built round three sides, with an overgrown saluting base and a military chapel forming the fourth. Rows and rows of small windows were covered with rusted steel grilles, blank eyes gummed up with the imprisonment of history.

In the morning the whole square was deserted, the corners of the buildings leaning out in sharp shadows threatening one another. At the very edge of the rock, the smaller houses of officers' quarters crumbled amongst clumps of green singing with cicadas. The sky behind was flat blue, taking away all perspective like a bad painting.

Inside the buildings, narrow steps led into long empty rooms, the walls covered in drawings of crumbling saffron and chocolate, men with huge dark moustaches leading donkeys through desert landscapes isolated with palm trees. The faces fell into sagging looks of disappointment where the plaster had rotted.

Leading off the main rooms, looking on to the sea through gaps behind barbed wire and boarding, small ante-chambers covered with cobwebs were scrawled with pencil marks—drawings of tanks, faces, and names with missing letters rubbed out like casualties.

Over the doorways were numbers, and above them signs saying "*Chambre du Capitaine*" and "*Section Commandant*". Inside were crossed flags and the words "*Honneur et Patrie*". Over the rooms hung a heavy humid atmosphere, with the wind blowing in off the sea, so that doors banged and shutters flapped about.

Round the fortress itself a narrow wall marked the edge of the rock, from where, looking over, the sea broke up in white frustration and no visible support for the fort could be seen.

A few yards in, scrubs of grass grew haphazardly back from the rock, creating a waste that was filled with dumps of rotting food, rusty tins, and pieces of twisted steel.

Over the mouth of the inlet, observation posts were built into the rock or else stood up from stone gutted clumps, the turrets collapsed and pointing out to sea like machine-guns.

A cemetery stood on the cliff's edge, a miniature Moroccan town glinting from pinnacles, and smooth white tombstones—flowers were laid red against them in gashes of new blood.

Out at sea a small sailing boat blew about, as haphazardly as a slip of paper.

.   .   .   .   .

52

BONIFACIO

A solitary gendarme walks across the empty parade ground, and up beyond the chestnut trees to the gendarmerie where clothes hang from a top window fluttering white in the breeze as though in surrender. Down the cobbled alleyways swarms of flies are thick over festering rubbish.

Small dark-eyed children, barefoot, play at the doors of the cave houses. By the offices of *Le Petit Marseillais*, "*Votez Oui ou Non*" is scrawled up in letters of dark magenta with below it "*Vive D-AI——*", the last word splashed and disfigured with drips of the paint falling to the ground like blood.

Outside the Café de la Poste, at a table sheltered by trees, the Paris papers give out their current news—a girl of fourteen has killed her mother with an axe in Toulon, women prisoners went mad as they were burnt to death in Fresnes prison, a scandal over Government contracts breaks in Washington.

Through the small tunnel from the port below and just over the drawbridge, a donkey struggles in the heat, laden with vegetables, sacks, and fruit, a man on his back, and flies in a halo round his head.

The cicadas croak, and shirts stick to men's backs in the damp heat.

An old man, his face weather beaten till it is the colour of charcoal, and grimed with a beard, rests on the step of the *Parti Communiste Français*. A thousand years crumble in the flat stone parapets over his head. The postcards on the stalls say all the information he does not need—about the Templar Church of San Domenico, the Pisan Occupation, the days of the Genoese Republic, the attack by Alfonso and the heroism of the women, the garrison under Napoleon. The children read the postcards like unwanted history books and throw away the dates in their memory. The festering flies and the slogans on the wall are more important.

A girl carrying a pail of water climbs the steep, dark staircase up from the street, her blue shorts pale against the deep brown of her thighs. A boy in a red and white jersey spins a top.

Under blue placards marked "*Visites aux Grottes*" men sit smoking pipes, waiting for passengers for the boat trip to the grottoes. On the narrow inlet of green water a red motor-boat vamps the sun's eye.

Later, in the cool church with effigies coloured like sweets and chairs turned upside down like a restaurant at closing time, black-shawled women touch themselves with Holy Water and crouch, kneeling and making their simple devotions. On the walls signs are written up "Do not spit or bring dogs inside this sacred place". "Do not talk or behave with disorderliness. This is the house of your blessed creator."

The women cross themselves and through the open door the sunlight touches them in golden accolades. From the street the smell of stale urine mingles with the incense and the priest walks interminably up and down outside—a lost Captain on a landlocked bridge.

.   .   .   .   .

Over a hill and a break in the rocks a small bay was hidden out of sight from the port. The narrow path that led to it was built up with stones the colour of white, bleached bones and on either side thick clumps of fir and *maquis* pressed their perfume out in suffocating waves. Red butterflies flew up from the bushes, and across the stones black beetles moved with the clumsy inevitability of tanks. Lizards scrawled away from the noise into new patches of burning sun.

Then the path fell in a string-coloured drop into the cove. By the sea's edge a boy and a girl painted an upturned boat, and around them men worked building a stone wall round a small garden. Children jumped naked out of small boats and dived onto the seaweed floor, emerging brown and shining with the glitter of water. The sand, pressed under foot, became black, and all afternoon the waves lisped in a soft effeminate threnody.

.   .   .   .   .

The shadows grew longer, the houses washed in a peach bloom as the sun fell behind the fortress like a coin magnetised into the water. By their boats men sat in rows weaving the straw strongholds of lobster pots, their hands moving with the assurance of blind men reading, their eyes drifting.

Up on the hillside, through a pergola of vine and figs, the small lights of the restaurant played out over flower beds and stone verandahs. On the tables were tomatoes, lobsters, whiting, great bowls of soup, cheese and wine.

The cicadas oscillated through the heat. Below on the waterfront, lights winked out from navigational beacons, and occasionally the headlamps of lorries travelling over mountains dipped down onto the water.

PROPRIANO

LEAVING Bonifacio the feeling of history dissolves. The deep ravines of nearly dry river beds twist in snake-skin scrawls, trying all the time to get away from the raised paws of the cactus and being turned back by the roads, always the road hedging them off like policemen herding the scrawny falls of water down the main channel into the sea.

The road itself climbs immediately, circling the gradient diagonally and then round and round till it reaches the summit—so cars and buses seen coming up seem like slow clumsy imitations of Wall of Death riders—only there is no harsh cylinder of noise, as all the exhaust and revving is drained up by the landscape's silences and invisible threads seem to be drawing the cars along deafly into the blank of the sky.

At moments the road twists westward, so that chinks of sea like patches of blue skin appear from below and great grey rocks whittled into slate effigies stand up transfixed from the coastline. Then the road branches inland again, up over La Tonnara and over the bed of the Ventilegne River.

The humps of scrub grow sharper, with ledges of honey-coloured rock hanging in tiers over the route, perfect observation posts for bandits to come riding down from in a sudden flail of dust and loose stones to block the way out. But the *mise en scène* is too theatrical, too obviously dramatic to leave anything left for man to do. The over-charged, picture-postcard beauty is self-fulfilled, with nothing for the mind to work on—the cactus, the stone-gashed ledges, the dark green skyline like a temperature chart against the over-blue of the sky itself and below, a drop in Time, the sea—all these say what they mean, death, passion, jealousy, struggle, over and over again, so that the whole jagged emotionalism of the utterance becomes breathless and then monotonous when it is apparent that the symbols have no more meaning. They are statements, holding out promises of action that are never fulfilled or that have been fulfilled so often in the past that they have grown tired of making their gestures.

North of Caldarello clumps of forest break up the inscrutability of rock and then near the top of the gradient, built into the mountain itself, Sartène hangs on a wide ledge; from a distance the fawn church

57

like a message of refuge seems to stretch stone arms out round the houses dropping down the hill, gathering them into its embrace.

But nearer, the face seems to have fallen, the town slipped out of the grasp of the holy arms. Houses with gaping faces staring out of windows, pavements deep with refuse, petrol pumps, boarded-up shops on either side of the road and everywhere the rusty tin trappings of garages and fantastic unreal advertisements, speak of the desultory apathy of semi-commercialised living—the chromium without the polish, the smart café name over a filth-laden doorway, the political scrawls on the houses written up as though they were charms against evil. But no activity, no effort anywhere.

The street breaks into a sudden wide square with chestnut trees, their leaves swinging like green star-fishes, and then slides off the spine of the hill down between vines across the Rixxanese.

At the foot the first few symbols of Propriano, an old car chassis, bits of twisted mudgards, a rusted, dripping water tap and timber strewn about in sheds hold up the road with their dead weight of decay.

.   .   .   .   .

The town itself is divided into two; the handful of shops round the main street, neglected and stained that are tilted on the hillside, and the port façade that turns down in a "T" along the shore to the left, while the road to Olmeto and Ajaccio breaks back into the mountains.

The coast is lined with strips of very white sand which because of the bathing bring in a few tourists in the summer, and at the extreme point a white lighthouse rises above the rocks in an assertion of purity. The same mauve tents of hills shut in the bay with over-bearing closeness—huge faces so close their breath burns over the festering little port at their feet, breaking its will and hammering in its insignificance.

The shore road is littered with cafés perched over rickety jetties, hotels with stairways slopped over with vegetable ends rotting amongst discarded cigarettes, dirty children sitting abjectly on pavements, hubs of wheels thrown over geranium bushes, and piled along the beach, by miniature rail-tracks, thick grey pencils of timber.

A haphazard concession to tourists is a shack by the rocks marked "LIDO" with grey wooden tables round the edge, overlooking the water and a gramophone in the bar playing continuously, rumbas and tangos, that float out over the sand hills where German prisoners work on laying fresh lines to the timber sheds.

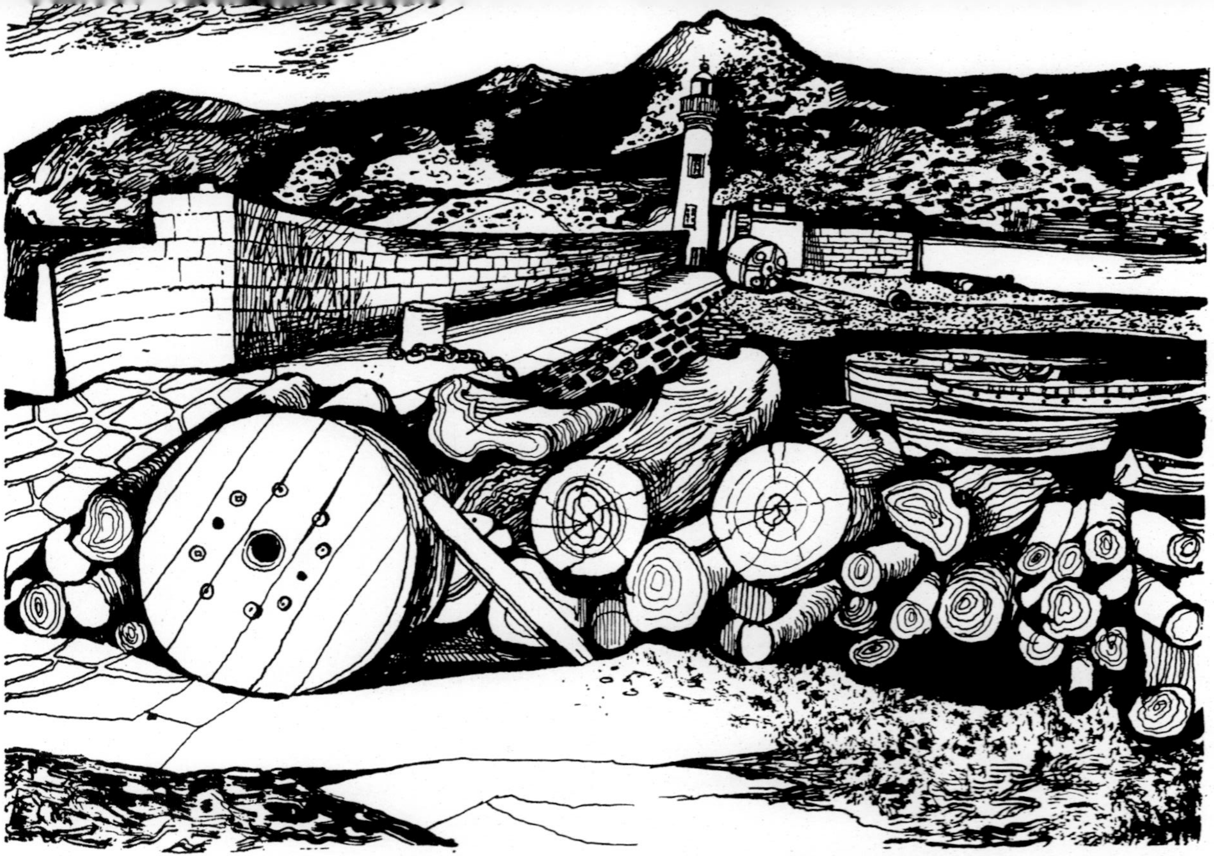

PROPRIANO—TIMBER AND LIGHTHOUSE

Timber and fishing provide the town's livelihood, where life has not been contaminated by neglect and the corruption of tourists.

.   .   .   .   .

Evening with its softness toned down the harshness of the squalor. The refuse became indistinguishable from shadows and the stained walls fell into quadrants of muted light. The corner place, with over its awnings "*A bas Thorez le déserteur*" and across the street in large blood-coloured letters "*Un seul chef de Gaulle*", was lightly coated with people sitting drinking *pastis*, and at a first glance the hopeless, apathetic expressions might have been taken for the ordinary content of relaxation.

The red and white chairs of the *chi-chi* Alaska Bar were laid out on the shore and ice clinked in apéritif glasses where a dozen or so tourists from Paris—men in red jerseys and shorts, tall blonde girls in rolled up trousers and pale blue or green-striped shirts—sat about drinking, with the huge hills by Castello del Corvo over the water in front of them and a bell of light stretching over the bay from the lighthouse.

It was possible to forget the dark filth hidden in the doorways next to the cold light of the Alaska, the small windows with unwashed faces peering out from them as if they were ghettoes, the desolation in the old women sitting on the narrow iron bridges that joined the houses in the back alleyways—where the sidewalks were filled with human ordure and flies swarmed over them like plagues.

From the Lido the rumba music came sliding over the water with its fragrance and nostalgia, its conjuring up of old hopeless desires that had led nowhere. The shaded lights on the dance floor changed from green to sober orange, the rhythm softly and insistently propelling the couples in broken lunges in and out of each other's thoughts. A frieze of people sat round the tables, the sea coming up all round.

The suffering, the jagged edges of bad smells, the stupid avidity of people, had been transformed as if by art into a pattern where beauty dominated every reaction, a conjurer whose hands soothed away all questions with "This is the real world, the other is only imaginary", and people are drugged into acceptance, throwing overboard their cargoes of worry and fear. Then in the morning the known world pushes through the stone houses, seeping into the daylight.

From the windows in shacks and tenements the faces stared dumbly outwards—passengers in a lost train lighted up at night, for whom the landscape, their view, always moved, but they themselves never.

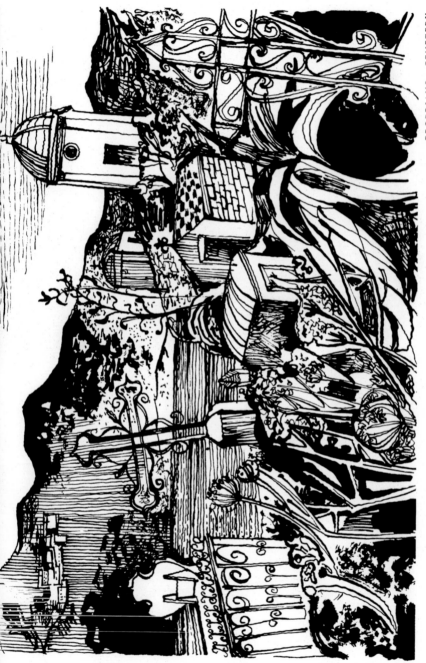

In the hotel bedroom the mosquitoes flew in and out of the lace curtains, and later, waking up, the sheets were dotted in the turned-on light with fat, blood-burdened fleas, lying still as ink or slowly waddling over the stained islands of other people's love. The night was absolutely airless, the silence only broken by heavy breathing in the room behind the narrow partitions.

"Le Plus Corse des Corses."

WHEN SAMPIERO landed just north of Propriano in the Gulf de Valenco early in June 1564 he was already famous as the greatest patriot in the island and the most feared by the Genoese.

His hatred of Genoa had largely been kindled by his unjustified imprisonment on his return home to Bastelica after his marriage in France with Vannina d'Ornano, the daughter of a wealthy nobleman. Sampiero himself was of low birth but had had a distinguished career in the French Army and had returned a Colonel after long service under Francis I and in the Medici.

When the French resumed their efforts to drive the Genoese out of Corsica, Sampiero led the attack on Bastia, which fell very quickly, and then took Corte and all the surrounding mountain district.

At the last moment the Genoese managed to get help from Spain and Germany, and under Andreas Doria re-landed at San Fiorenzo. Although they re-took Bastia, they never gained a real stranglehold on the island and in 1556 a truce was signed leaving the government in French hands. But any hopes of a stabilised Corsican Constitution were destroyed only three years later when, by the Treaty of Cateau-Cambrésis, Corsica was given back to the Bank of San Giorgio and from them to the Genoese.

Sampiero made every effort to organise help on behalf of Corsican independence but finally—after having killed his wife whom he thought was under the spell of Genoa—he came back himself with only a few friends, made the landing off Propriano, and advanced through the mountains gathering volunteers. Again he took Corte, and later Vescovato, where he fought a pitched battle with the Genoese. Re-inforcements had to be sent out by Genoa, and when General Stephen Doria arrived he began a cold-blooded, calculated laying waste of the island. Bastelica, Sampiero's birthplace, was destroyed as a symbol, farms and villages were burnt, and hostages taken.

But Sampiero, without any help from France, refused to give in and eventually drove Doria out. In his place General Fornari was sent out, and, through the treachery of his own servant, Sampiero was lured into the narrow pass of Cavro. An ambush was laid and though he fought for hours against great odds, Sampiero was killed by a shot in the back. His son Alfonzo escaped in the middle of the battle and came back to carry on the struggle for two years after his father's death. An honourable peace was made in 1568 and comparative quiet was restored for a few years under the Governorship of George Doria.

THE WINDLESS afternoon hung over the low coast road that went up through the "T" of the town and then over the curve at the cliff's edge to the shore below. The sea was pale green where it broke, ribbed further out with darker strips as a floor of rock and seaweed shadowed it.

The cemetery lay overlooking the estuary, a blistered counterpoint to the town, with its domes and turreted vaults rising out of cactus, and occasionally faded red flowers lying against the graves.

Then in an arc round the shore tall green reeds lay like hair styles ruffled with wind, leaning back from the sea and beyond, over the white bridge, the olive groves reached up the throat of the hill.

The path upward snaked through overhanging branches wrapped over the skeleton fingers of brown earth that formed the hillside. The ground itself was laid with jagged white stones, a mouth of crooked teeth curling round the slope of the gradient, trying to get a grip. From the stones lizards ran out for shelter like people in an air-raid, then finding their way blocked dashed back into cover. Red butterflies glazed through the blue light and for the first time birds shook out the early autumn from the *maquis* so that leaves draped the path's edge with rust.

At the top of the hill, five miles up, a disused tower became an objective for the climbing eye, a citadel that had to be taken.

The track spread round isolated vineyards, partridge surfacing from the sea of dark foliage and shots breaking up against the blank silence of the rocks. The path was covered with twigs and stems camouflaged into pieces of string or snakes concussed with the siege of heat. Heavy black beetles wobbled like out of date tanks in foreign territory.

The white tower became obscured with olives and the track half ran out amongst small firs, then found itself again like a dog picking up the scent and plunging into undergrowth.

What did the tower stand for ? Hope, power, a landing stage for the journey over the horizon where new conditions of life would open up, and the slate of the past be washed clean ? Perhaps only a momentary halt out of the reach of oppression, a breathing space in a No-Man's Land where on either side the dangers and the fear waited, but which in

65

itself was a refuge, a Church without a Christ that demanded no lip service and was free to any man.

The sun's shadows created angular extensions of the trees, strange grasping shapes that seemed frozen into timelessness at the ugliest moment of their reflection. Then the path broke suddenly out of the hill and, below, the olive groves stretched out in belts to the sea, fringed with the light green of the reeds and behind them, dotted with dark copses, the opposite peaks tied up the mauve hills.

The narrow slits of the tower grew into sight again, and into arm's length; over its shoulder Olmeto straggled out of the rock, three ledges of houses with water falling from a fountain and the sun pink on its back.

.   .   .   .   .

Olmeto had a church, a school and a public lavatory. Avenues of people were sitting on either side of the main street—the middle of the three ledges—which tilted up into the sky at an angle of forty-five degrees.

It was Sunday night and the café tables filled with green *pastis* glasses and people growing out of the twilight—bearded shepherds with eyes of olives, pomaded young men with advertisement hair, in white shirt-sleeves, middle-aged women grinning out of their gapped mouths, an Italian tenor weeping over their heads from a radio loudspeaker.

In a little dark room near the inn—a fire burning in the grate—soup was brought with coarse bread, fried eggs and tomatoes, white cheese and bottles of pure, iced wine. Two gendarmes sat eating at the only other table and hovering like a mother in the background, the wrinkled grey-haired old *patronne* watched over the meal, silently clasping and unclasping her gnarled fingers. In the street the voice of Tino Rossi played out from cracked, over-used records.

Later, in the shade of the rock, there was dancing with a cement playground for floor and flags hanging out in streamers from a pole in the middle. Small children sat at the foot of the rock half asleep on the women's laps, and over the dancers—girls in black or cheap, brightly-coloured frocks, men in shirts glowing against the brown of their skin—the music came out like a message from God, blurred by the ceaseless shuffle of the *paso doble*.

At a buffet, glasses of red *Cap Corse* were lined up and whisked away on trays to the tables in the darkness where voices rose and fell, not listening to the music, and political slogans were bandied about, de Gaulle, the Communists, Ramadier, Blum, Marshall—while on the

66

OLMETO

dance floor the girls shuffled round with each other like empty seats in hurdy-gurdies at a fair ground.

High up in the top cluster of houses, a silence in the spills of light, the house where Merimée's *Colomba* had died, lay guarded by ilex trees.

After midnight when the dancing stopped, it was as though a ray of light from the future had been put out and the mountain-side returned to the primitive timelessness of its way of life, a Cinderella for whom the *paso dobles* and the tangos, the Dubonnet advertisements and the wedge shoes, were put away at the stroke of the clock.

The moon came out and the air was full of the quiet of olives.

THREE CONTEMPORARY BIOGRAPHIES

ROBERTO OLIVIERI was forty-seven and gold-toothed, the stubble of his chin like cheese round the cut grin of his cunning. Daily he drove the mountain bus into the ravines and valleys of the Taravo down into Ajaccio, and back over the Rixxanese to Santa Lucia di Tallano.

He brought with him cigarettes from the ships at Ajaccio,distributing them in the Black Market at Olmeto, Viggiannello, Propriano and Santa Lucia at prices rising in a crescendo according to the distance away, 25 francs, 50 francs, 75 francs, 100 francs for packets of twenty Naja's bought on board ship at 8fr.50. There was no other form of cigarette distribution in the south of the island.

Oliviero had fought at the tail end of the Great War and been wounded by shrapnel in the leg, so he limped about with the exaggerated air of a sailor—home after his last ship, his memory trophied with exotic ports and women in waterfront cafés. To complete the portrait which he secretly liked to perpetuate, he kept his peaked driver's cap on the side of his head, only taking it off, for some reason, when he relieved himself.

Actually, apart from three weeks on the Western Front, he had never been out of Corsica, but he had seen a great many films in Ajaccio that had fired his imagination.

At night he beat on the tables of the café emphasising crude political points, bellowing against the Communists, leering at Ramadier, enthusiastic over Bevin, and adoring de Gaulle. That was his one integrity and his only constant love.

Pierrot Viale, slim, dark-skinned, his eyes set deep and serious in the cave of his face, always looked deeply at people, silent for a few moments before speaking. Then his voice was quiet and authoritative, his eyes flowering slightly in the frills of their jet pupils.

He had been back home only a few months after two and a half years in the French Navy, a wireless operator in a submarine that had carried special passengers to North Africa before the Allied landings. During those years he had been ashore at Algiers, Gibraltar, New York, Plymouth; he had a passing acquaintance with the brothels of Toulon, Marseilles, and the near brothels of Villefranche. But they had not

69

ROBERTO OLIVIER

PIERROT VIALE

altered his reserve of manner, his serious appraisal of small-talk exchanges, his air of living always well within his capabilities.

The past had already become a book from which he occasionally repeated phrases as if amused that they really related to him. He was a Socialist by instinct, but took no part in the political clamour that wasted itself round him.

Every morning he went down at sunrise to the olive groves round the lower slopes of the hillside, some bread, sausage, cheese and wine in a basket. And every evening as it grew dark he came up the hill again, ate the dinner his mother had got ready for him and read aloud in the room with white lace curtains.

His life was already ordained, part of the mountain, and as regular as sunset or the seasons.

Dominique Santucci, smiling, with a slick cocksure manner, good teeth and handsome in a slightly greasy, already plumpish way, was orphaned at fifteen, the eldest of three brothers, each five years younger than the other.

Now twenty, he had for five years run single-handed the small inn which had belonged to his grandfather. So he had grown confident, forced into self-dependence, tough but generous in all his relationships.

Monthly he took the bus into Ajaccio and came back with new dance records for his radiogram loudspeaker, and illustrated papers from France and America.

In six months he would go for his military service first to Marseilles, then probably to Dakar, leaving his brother in charge of the inn and the youngest child still at the village school.

Perhaps then, if the illustrated papers became real, he would stay in France or go to England or America and be a waiter, saving up there for the day when he could retire and buy property, an olive grove or a vineyard while his brother looked after the inn.

But that would be a long time ahead, and the picture palace, the dance hall, the smart chromium bar, the different people—he wanted these symbols to become actual in the meantime.

So he read his papers in between serving drinks behind the bare board that served as a bar, and smiled, thinking all the time of the glamourised world outside, taking no part in politics, aloof from all ties.

And the village of old people and young children would see him, like so many others, only for a few days each year, till middle-age was over—their absence accepted by the young girls and the old women as something to be expected, the loss every year of the men who would not return till it was too late.

72

DOMINIQUE SANTUCCI

HOMECOMING

Coming down to Ajaccio in a morning of mackerel skies was almost like coming home. The stalls were all up in the markets, the stale sweat of the night washed over with the heavy perfume of peaches and melons, the sidewalks littered with over-ripe fruit and the newsboys calling out "*L'Intransigeant, Le Monde, Paris-Presse*".

A Greek cargo boat was unloading on the quay, and hanging round the gangways the middle-men worked their rackets while the fishermen laid out their nets for cleaning and the flying boat came in over the water from Tunis.

The outside world had re-established its links. It became a curious sensual experience, a massaging into life of the more civilised senses, to watch the tables being laid out in the Solferino, the shops suddenly very modern, the newspapers only two days old, the streets nearly full with smart women in coloured slacks and jerseys, men sitting about at cafés drinking coffee and reading *L'Espoir de Nice* with pictures of film stars on holiday at Cannes, theatre news from Paris, urgent headlines of economic disaster sandwiched between adultery cases and suicides.

In the hotel *Madame* grinned from her expensive mouth, while the Russian doorman continued his story about the betrayal of Karl Marx. The stair walls had been distempered, otherwise everything was the same, with the lavatory still blocked up. Lunch was produced out-of-doors with squashed melons strewn about the road like trampled flowers and the cranes moving against the background of pale sea, with sailing boats loitering about by the Sanguinares and dockhands squatting in the shade of the palm trees on the square by the greening war memorial.

In the cafés there was the usual disembarkation crowd of travellers, men sitting about in Palm Beach suits, ship's officers in white drill and the port itself galvanised into motion like some robot wound up every boat day, running down when there were no ships in.

By midday the harbour was full—the *Ville d'Ajaccio* and the *Katoomba* had come in together overloaded with passengers from the Middle East en route for Marseilles, and the bars were jostled with strange,

LANDSCAPE NEAR AJACCIO

artificial women coolly draping their feminine authority over sweating middle-aged business men.

The regulars, in slightly dirtier tropical suits, eyed them with a sort of contemptuous pity—men with interesting expressive faces, good clothes become shabby, the clockwork that ran their lives having suddenly grown tired, and left them like sea-wrack in this or that port almost out of the civilised world. In this or that way the tension had snapped which could take them back to families, jobs, countries. Instead they existed, slightly shopsoiled, but with the air of having been gentlemen, characters grouped about by a novelist—a Frenchman, a Greek, an Englishman, a few Egyptians—who had been told of the plot and needed no rehearsing of their parts, hugging some strange disenchantment that was only drugged into a flicker of life when a boat came in. What lay, one wondered, behind the unmade bedroom in the second-class hotel—besides the emptied bottles, the month-old papers sent out from home, the faded photographs of genteel women?

The crowds moved about, their eyes pecking at the shops, their noses scenting out restaurants suitable for their positions, children trailing after men in topees, their wives in wide-brimmed straw hats—and the sun beating down over the filthy sidestreets, the gendarme directing the traffic with smooth-gloved gestures in the Cours Napoléon, the black-shawled women sitting on the floors of their hovels like down-at-heel, passed-over nuns.

Wʜᴀᴛ ɪs there to say about a town once history has dried up in it and only a sickly trickle of existence like pus still runs through it ?

Corte looked as if the nerve that gave it life had gone dead, leaving it a bare shell of buildings devoid of feeling to carry on a pretence of life-as-before. The great Gothic fortress stood on a small loaf-shaped hill, behind which the taller skyline of mountains spread as far as the eye could see in hostile ramparts.

So the town itself had the appearance of being seen through a stereoscope, sticking out in relief from the pasteboard background of hills.

Down from the citadel—almost obscured amongst overgrown rock— the older buildings hung down in tiers, pink-washed houses with ugly brown stains, dirty tenements with rusted balconies overloaded with washing and, from amongst them, the square turret of the church trying to push itself clear of the filth.

In the evening sun it was like one of those vistas of suburban slums seen from a passing train—the softening, pastel shades of light falling across steep narrow alleyways cobbled with refuse, the children sitting about dirty and bare-footed on the doorsteps of the airless dark houses, the dilapidation of the soul seeping out in the damp acid stains on walls.

The whole edifice is pincered between two rivers, but they were pitiful, scanty trickles running under curved bridges—from where, far below, women could be seen washing clothes, remarkably clear and accentuated against the landscape by the purity of the air, so that they were complete movements.

Tacked on to the west of the hill, on a sort of table all on its own, the newer part of the town seemed to be disowning all knowledge of the garbage on its left. Long modern-looking blocks of flats, yellow and white, with squat villas along roads punctuated with palm trees and geraniums formed little areas of gentility which housed passing business men, government officials, and various better-class function- aries who were forced to break their journey between Ajaccio and Bastia. The streets were cleaner and wider with little squares in them that had nothing to do with history, and shuttered windows that seemed to be drawn as if denying the sweat-grimed *maquillage* of the fallen city in front of them.

On the other wing, nearer the citadel, lay the inclining streets of the official part of the old town—the Mairie, the crumbling old officers' quarters, government blocks, and in the Place Paoli the huge stone statue of the great General with its faded lettering—"*La Corse reconnaissante*"—looking out over the arid river-beds and the dingy streets slobbering into the valley below.

.   .   .   .   .

The fortress was originally built by the Moors early in the eighth century, becoming subsequently the residence of Saracen Kings, and the seat of successive Genoese, French and English governments.

But, for the enormous amount of history, treachery, battles and legislation that had issued forth from it, it did not seem a remarkably impressive place, nor in fact very large.

The same air of derelict hopelessness hung over it as over the garrison buildings of Bonifacio—but here no sense or legacy of past achievement transmitted itself. The paths up to the top were all overgrown, the bushes that had sprung over them dotted with rusted bits of steel, and it looked more than anything else like a toy fort that a sadistic child had kicked about and then left lying around.

At the eastern end of the actual citadel two small rounded turrets half hang over the rock and below them the walls fall sheer down in jagged perpendicular stoniness—the same walls on which in 1746 the son of the Corsican general Gaffori, who had been captured by the Genoese, was hung down alive as a last resort to stem the fire made by his father's troops. But the general ordered the attack to go on and the fortress fell, with his son uninjured. Seven years later the General himself, through the connivance of his illegitimate brother, was murdered by the Genoese.

It was the same pathetic story of treachery that runs all through Corsican history—the fierce pride of independence, the refusal to admit defeat and the great long periods of struggle against oppression broken only by some stab in the back from a traitor within. Symbolically, the clocks in the garrison had all stopped at different times, as if they were pointing the hours of betrayal, inhuman hands that relentlessly exhibited their moral laws, saying "Do not forget" and engraving the picture of the clock face on to the memory of everyone who saw it.

CORTE—THE OLD TOWN AND FORTRESS

EXILES

NOT FAR from where, ironically enough it seemed, Corsica had been proclaimed part of the British Empire in 1794, the block of buildings that had housed the English garrison troops was now filled with German working parties.

They came up the hill, stripped to the waist, their green caps faded with sun and sweat, and picks on their backs—up to the compound where a solitary goalpost stood in the middle of a rough stone square.

They had been there two years, said the young *Lager Kommandant*, a young blond German with typical long hair falling over his face and shorts turned up almost to the tops of his thighs.

He had been an engineering student in Saarbrücken before the war and had been able to travel about learning languages, so they had made him *Lager Kommandant* and interpreter because he could speak French—and so he was excused going on the working parties or down to the quarries and the roads below.

He had been taken prisoner at Marseilles and sent straight over to Corte. Once a month he received letters from home; but there were no radio or papers in the camp. The inner tubing of their football had burst and they couldn't get another one; and they were not allowed out of the precincts of the fortress. Only, occasionally from the caretaker who lived at the entrance lodge, he learned something of what was going on in the world outside.

But about events in Corte he was well informed. "Since I have been here," he said gloatingly but with a naïve enjoyment of it all, "there have been sixteen people shot dead in the town. The Vendetta is officially over, perhaps, but a kind of unconstitutional law operates when people come riding down from the hills"—and he pointed to all the shacks on the mountain-sides—"and because of vengeance or political intrigue started by family quarrels, they pick out their victims and then ride off again. The body lies there till the flies get at it and nothing is done officially because it is so difficult to get to the bottom of the matter. So it fades away till the next time and for a few days there is talk. But nothing is done about it.

"Then a few months ago a French corporal, whose girl friend worked in the pay office of the supply depot, got the key from her and disappeared with 200,000 francs. They tried to blame that on the Germans," he said, "but since we shall be here for another few years it's not likely that it would be much use to us."

He grinned, showing white teeth from a prematurely aged face, the eyes gone dead as if there were no batteries inside that could make them keep pace with the mouth, and held out his hand, saying:

"Danke, auf Wiedersehen," before going back into the deathless cemetery of the citadel.

"Inglese, c'erana i nostri amici; ma non le sono più"

Because patriotism is a currency that has been so depreciated—mixed up with propaganda and totalitarian ideologies, half-way between a sort of genteel outmoded jingoism and the rubber truncheon of the fascist thug—it is difficult to re-create the particular quality of national belief that must have driven a man like Paoli. But the man himself—a strong, honest face with fair regular features—dressed in green and gold habits, who made a practice of studying faces often for minutes on end before feeling compelled to relax his expression, who through one treachery after another still preserved the belief that ultimately Right would prevail, crystallised in his own personality a particular aspect of Corsican history.

He was more or less born into a position of leadership, for his father Giacinto had been one of the great Corsican patriots exiled to Naples for stirring up resistance to the Genoese.

Pascal Paoli had, at the age of fourteen, gone with his father into exile, and in Naples he attended the Academy, went to court, studied literature and languages, and became an officer.

He spent nearly thirteen years at Naples, learning the art of government and acquiring such a reputation that the Corsicans repeatedly sent over requests for him to come home and take over command of the Army and the Administration.

Finally, at his elder brother Clemens' invitation, Paoli landed at Aleria in April 1755. By July a document had been drawn up at the will of the people making him "economical, political and general chief" and giving him authority "to command over this Kingdom with full power, except when there shall be occasion to consult upon matters concerning the state, which he cannot treat of without the concurrence of the people, or their respective representatives".

Having himself become the State, Paoli set up a Government and made Corsica a Republic. The Genoese were still in possession of a large part of the island, but Paoli having at last provided a unifying symbol for the Corsicans, they made their first properly combined attack and succeeded in driving the Genoese out.

Immediately, Paoli set in motion laws for the establishment of order.

He created a Consulta, with representatives from each thousand of the people and they elected annually nine members to a Supreme Council. He substituted a system of legal justice for the Vendetta, which in its assumption of the right of private revenge had caused about 800 murders a year.

At Paoli's instigation a standing army was established with military instruction for all men over sixteen years of age; a university at Corte was opened, and schools set up in every village. Gradually agriculture and commerce were developed, and for the first time in Corsican history the cultivation of manners and the arts was evident amongst the people.

All this was accomplished during intermittent skirmishes with the Genoese, who finally getting sick of a losing battle, sold out to France. French troops then attacked the island and though Paoli held out for some time, he was forced to surrender after the battle of Ponte Nuova in May 1769.

The day before Louis XV assumed the sovereignty of Corsica, Paoli left for England, all his achievements undone, his hopes of stability and independence destroyed. What he had undertaken without violence, he was forced to give up through pressure of arms.

So without having any of the common characteristics Paoli became what constituted almost a revolutionary in exile. But he was only a revolutionary by circumstance and not by nature—his aims throughout had been the preservation of order, constitutional authority, and natural economic development.

Paoli spent several years in England and did not return to France till after the Revolution. He was stirred there by the extravagance of the purges in Paris, and his attacks on the Revolutionaries eventually caused him to be outlawed on grounds of treason.

However, encouraged by Paoli, the Corsicans achieved a secession from France and elected him President. Paoli then offered the island to the English Crown and in June 1794 it was proclaimed part of the British Empire, after minor battles with the French.

But difficulties grew up between the newly appointed Governor and Paoli, as a result of which Paoli retired and came back to London at the request of George III.

He had been only a short while in England when Corsica had to be evacuated, hastily and untidily, under pressure from French troops. Napoleon claimed the island of his birth in his name as a Frenchman.

Once again, and for the last time, the efforts of a Corsican to achieve a stabilised government under a Corsican administration had been undermined at the very moment when success seemed certain.

MICHELINE TO BASTIA

THE MICHELINE to Bastia was the great event of the day in the railway station at the foot of the hill. When it was due to arrive crowds of officials congregated on the thin strip of stone that served as a platform and waved it up the hill as though cheering a runner on the last lap of a race.

Compared with the awe with which everyone had spoken of it, it was a strange-looking object—a solitary carriage like an underground compartment, divided into two, with some thirty or so occupants in each side. But it was at once noticeable that the passengers were of a slightly higher social standing than those in the previous day's Rocket—there was in fact no third-class in this.

A few people got out, two Franciscans who must have been going up to the monastery that stood behind the town, and a handful of tourists, business men and gendarmes.

In the train were several nuns, Capuchines, French military and naval officers as well as a number of sedate-looking families, all sitting up straight and reading newspapers or talking, not looking unlike passengers going from Montparnasse to the Madeleine in the Paris Metro.

The railway this time ran through much flatter country, soft, almost English hills with young vines looking like fields of cabbages from a distance. The track zig-zagged between occasional high ridges, moving eastward through Francardo, the rails bisected by white paths which ran up slopes dotted with cattle. At each road junction the driver blew a horn on the Micheline, a deep rich klaxon full of its driver's authority.

After about an hour and a half the sea appeared behind low sand hills, deep blue under the same pale stare of sky that had never changed. The railway followed the coast, past long deserted beaches with white soft dunes ribbed and humped with scrawls of grass.

Close in to the shore three rusted ships lay gutted; two of them were askew with sea right up over their superstructure, but the third sat bolt upright in a few feet of water, like a surprised bather who had swum aground but refused to admit it, carrying on a private fiction that everything was still all right.

When Bastia came in sight, its first view unimpressively back-stage, the sun had grown sticky and the compartment had slumped a little, irritable with flies.

.   .   .   .   .

How seldom towns that have a past, that have been the subject of dreams and myths, live up to expectations. They are like those wonderful harbours first seen from the sea, picture postcards realised in stone

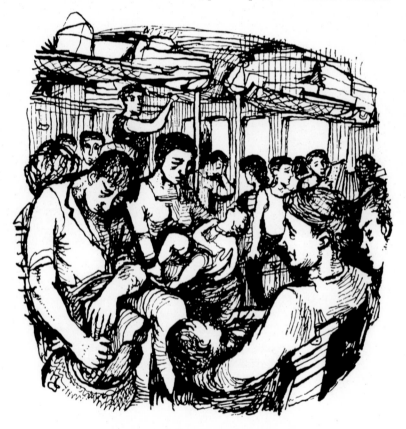

under too blue skies, which, when the ship ties up and the streets become streets to walk in, collapse like an illusion. Can this be the same place that we threw over our lives to come to?

Bastia had been represented as a prosperous, busy commercial port, with a great romantic past and a new harbour where boats came in weekly from Nice, a beautiful ancient city, that had grown with new buildings, squares and good shops.

But it seemed very different from that at first sight. Above all no one had said anything about the bombing, which in fact was the most noticeable thing about the town. The houses on either side of the road down from the station were pitted with shrapnel and shell marks, whole tops of buildings crumbling away like spittle into piles of dishevelled brick on the sidewalks. The buildings themselves all wore an air of semi-abasement, with people emerging from the ground floors but the upper windows glassless and black like opened mouths.

The road led down into a wide oblong space along the new harbour wall, an open square with a bandstand in the middle, and all up one side, looking onto the sea, the different coloured chairs, blue, pink and silver, of the cafés which formed a solid street.

But the square was almost deserted, a few desultory couples sitting about at tables with half-drained *pastis* glasses in front of them, and in the new harbour only the rusted masthead of a sunk ship broke the oily glassiness of the water.

The war had passed on, the armies gone northward, leaving only a few scrapheaps of iron, a debris of worn-out vehicles, an anachronistic sign or two, "U.S. Naval Officers' Club" painted on a wooden board, as evidence that they had ever really been there.

And it seemed as if with them they had taken the heart of the city.

.   .   .   .   .

Bastia is two towns shaped in a Greek "Є" with the sea on one side and the dark skyline of Monte Muzzone cutting it off on the other. The middle stroke of the "Є" forms the dividing line between the old and new harbours, and the two ways of existence, which are joined by the Boulevard Paoli at the back, are complete in themselves.

Each sector has its market place, its type of shops, its style of buildings. They share only the railway station and the Napoléon and Paris Cinemas which are next door to one another in the middle.

The new section has four or five widish streets, with tall yellow buildings in an already bad state of decay, a handful of restaurants with unprepossessing openings, and a disproportionate number of garages which tend to give the whole place the air of a back yard, but one which must at one time have been made for a respectably sized house. By the seafront it trails away into half-hearted goods sheds, small stony beaches with suburban-looking cafés perched on the road above them, and up the hill to the east, cork yards surrounded by olive and fig trees which stretch out to the village of Pietranera.

BASTIA—THE OLD PORT

But crossing from one harbour to the other is like crossing from one world to another. All pretence has been abandoned, and with it the ugly unsuccessful showiness that has never quite come off, is left on the other side.

Round a miniature dark green pool, which opens onto the sea between two lighthouses built at the two ends of the horseshoe, tiers of buildings rise up blue, pink, rust, grey—each with stairs dripping from the sore eyes of the windows, the brick collapsing so that it is impossible to tell whether it is decay or bomb damage.

Between the houses steep dark streets run under archways right up to the road that curls on the far side into the fortress itself and again open out into honeycombs of dingy black sidestreets.

Slightly higher than the rooftops, the two towers of Saint Jean-Baptiste stretch out their acid green campaniles, as if in answer to the huge coloured Ripolin advertisement that faces across it from the flat walls of the citadel.

On the quayside, boats with blistered colourings lie on the scum of water, and over it the reflection of the wall, draped with nets, moves sluggishly in the tide.

Right on the horizon the islands of Capraja and Elba loom out of the sea in dark masonried rocks.

.   .   .   .   .

At six o'clock the little three-piece orchestra outside the pale blue chairs of the Café L'Empire started up. L'Empire was a hideous building on the corner of a small street leading up from the Place St. Nicholas, garishly lit inside with a long chromium bar rail and absolutely empty. Its outside walls were painted white, with horizontal pink and green stripes that lit up at night with a harsh East-End vulgarity.

Each café up the Place, besides having its own colour of chairs, had its own loudspeaker, but a fairly uniform type of music was played in them all.

At different intervals after the "live" band, the loudspeakers were put on and, by seven-thirty or eight, each was going full blast, the arcs of their sound all intersecting so that from the middle of the square between the war memorial and a huge statue of Napoleon in a toga looking resolutely out towards Elba, it was possible to hear them all, without being able to listen to any. This was the most popular place, for the handful of tables that were occupied spread in a little semi-circle round the middle, with everybody looking as though some *spectacle* were just about to begin, for which all the

88

BASTIA—BOMB DAMAGE

hurdy-gurdying music from the cafés was nothing but a preliminary display.

But, as with the revolution, it would never materialise. The couples or families sat on till it grew dark and the lights came out on the hill above, neon over the sugared confectionery of L'Empire. The lighthouse beams travelled over the stilled water, the music went slavishly on, raucous and insensitive, and as the group of people began to disperse the trio petered out in a weak, noisy climax.

On the other side of the town, the lights in the old buildings glimmered like chandeliers in the windows of their decay, and the night came down over the piled rubbish with the smell of drains rising from the black hole of the basin.

BASTIA

Rain clouds had come up mysteriously during the night and by the time it was light a steady downpour had begun, with pencil-grey clouds covering the whole sky.

A few people were out in the streets, shopping in the Place Hotel de Ville where a row of fruit stalls were up, the fruit pinched and blighted like the faces of the women behind the counters. An enormous middle-aged woman drained off part of her mountainous breasts into the bored face of a child, dirty and covered in congealed sores. All the shops and public services had stopped. The library, cinemas, and restaurants were closed for the holiday.

The bell of Saint Jean-Baptiste tolled out over the market, and inside the church, priests moved about intoning amongst the fair-ground decorations of the altar, the voices coming faintly down to the almost deserted chairs where women in black sat bowed in silence.

The walls were covered with pink and yellow waxy Madonnas, and effigies of the Saints were arrested in the middle of symbolic narrative actions—as if an early amateur film had got stuck leaving the actors daubed and unreal in their exaggerated gestures.

A woman in grey fluttered her fan ceaselessly by the door; children with stained, running faces came in and crossed themselves with Holy Water, before darting out again, away from the lost voices rising and falling in their anaesthetic, and away from the hideous surroundings and the nearness of their God.

When the rain stopped, a voice started talking through the big loud-speaker in the Place St. Nicholas, a reminder of Corsican history with the repeated glory of Napoleon boomed out over the empty square, and the words of freedom and equality falling incongruously over the Emperor's statue.

Afterwards the "Marseillaise" was played over on a cheap record, and a few military tunes beat hopelessly at the flags on the war memorial.

Then they too were given up, and over chairs and upturned tables the rain came solidly down through the big palm trees.

Out at sea the islands were covered up in mist and a desertion like death hung over the whole port.

BASTIA—STREET SCENE

Theodor von Neuhoff

THE RAIN in the leaves outside the hotel window, the first really pure smell for days, and the sound of the church bell coming across the square had made it seem for a moment almost like England—a Sunday gone dead with nothing much to do.

There were only a few French papers about, two days old, and a book on Theodor von Neuhoff, the only crowned King of Corsica.

The story of Theodor's life, like his countryman Lassalle's, reads like one of those Hollywood films one knows could never come true— the orphaned student, the love affair and the duel, the flight to Paris and the foolish marriage. Then the desertion after the marriage had failed, the child and wife left without a word. Travel, financial speculations, meetings with political adventurers, finally a kingdom.

Yet Theodor had all this in reality, with periods of slavery at Algiers and a debtor's prison in London thrown in.

He appeared on the Corsican scene at a time when things were going extremely badly owing to lack of arms and money, and when there was little or no sense of unity amongst the people. All this Theodor was aware of, when he sent a letter to Domenico Rivarola, who was acting as Corsican plenipotentiary in Tuscany, saying that he could bring considerable material assistance to help in the fight against the Genoese, as well as possibilities of an alliance with several European powers. The one condition was that he should be made king.

Rivarola replied that if Theodor could produce proof of his claims, they would come to terms.

So in the spring of 1736 Theodor landed at Tavagna. His early life had been spent in Germany where he fought a duel with his best friend and killed him. Then he had left for France, been in the French Service, travelled in England, Holland and Spain, and had married.

Subsequently, tiring of his married life, he had returned to Paris and become involved with the Duke of Riperda and Cardinal Alberoni —acquiring in some curious underhand speculations a good fortune. He was later captured by the Moors on his way to Africa and put into slavery at Algiers.

94

But somehow or other he managed to bribe his way out, and with his money he bought arms and food at Tunis. From there he sent his letter to Rivarola.

Inmediately he had landed Theodor created a great impression. He had had the part worked out to perfection, the Turkish dress which suited him so handsomely, the retinue of French, Italian and Moorish attendants, the manners which he wore like gloves, the talk laced with the names of famous men, the promises—in a few days he had won the good graces of the influential leaders, Giafferi and Giacinto Paoli, and the date of his coronation was fixed.

On April 15th 1736, Theodor was crowned Theodor I of Corsica. His first steps were to build up public favour amongst the right people; so he at once created counts, marquises, and barons, in return for sums of money to be paid annually by the recipients. Special coins were struck, with on one side a shield wreathed with laurel under a crown marked "T.R.", and on the other "*Pro bono publico Re. Co.*".

At the same time Theodor personally took part in various actions against the Genoese, who had at first treated him with contempt as an impostor, but later became alarmed when his influence stiffened Corsican resistance and forced them to retreat into fortified towns, such as Bastia, which at once were put in a state of siege.

For eight months Theodor governed more or less successfully, reiterating all the time his promises of foreign support.

Eventually, when this showed no signs of arriving, a party of semi-opposition was formed by Paoli. Theodor's position grew uncomfortable and more or less to save his face he called his Parliament and announced that he intended to go in person to recruit help.

In the guise of a priest he landed at Leghorn and went up to Holland. For three years he bargained with merchants for loans and for arms. Finally he was able to sail for Aleria with a small fleet at the beginning of 1739.

Unfortunately for Theodor the French had taken possession of the island in his absence, and though he landed his cargo he did not dare to land himself, as the French General Boissieux had declared him an outlaw and every Corsican who joined him to be guilty of high treason.

But he did not give up. Four years later he reappeared with three British ships at Isola Rossa and a large number of supplies. His prolonged absence, however, had hopelessly weakened his position; as soon as he arrived he realised that nothing could now be done. He was greeted with hostility, so he turned straight back and returned to England.

His debts there had mounted so much that he was declared bankrupt and imprisoned. Horace Walpole exerted pressure on his behalf and enough money was raised to get him freed. But he died very soon afterwards and was buried in St. Anne's churchyard, Soho Square, where a plain monument was put at his head.

"Near this place is interred, Theodore, King of Corsica; who died in this parish, Dec: 11th, 1756, immediately after leaving the King's bench prison, by the benefit of the act of insolvency: in consequence of which, he registered his Kingdom of Corsica for the use of his creditors."

Theodor received the true Hays Office ending, yet the fantastic scenario of his existence contained little that was evil in itself. His intentions, in his highly personalised way, might have benefited Corsica as well as himself.

In the grey of the rainy afternoon, the leaves heavy with great silver drops and flies festooning the windows, Theodor seemed almost a message of love, a symbol of hope that had faded with the slow passage of time, leaving only the drab dejection that lay all around in the debris of another dead war.

GOD IS NOT MOCKED

By THE evening the rain had cleared up, leaving the air rinsed and the sea like green milk. The bells rang out from Saint Jean-Baptiste and the procession of Sainte-Marie emerged from the incense of the cathedral, moving down by the Hotel de Ville, into the Place St. Nicholas and up the hill again to the Old Port.

At the front, bearing banners like the sails of galleons, small boys in white formed a sort of figurehead behind which girls in their pale blue first Communion dresses, stretched back in long lines at either side of the street. In the middle walked priests, intoning at intervals, while snatches of responses drifted back from various parts of the procession. Solemn women in black shuffled along behind the girls, silent and grim-faced. Then more priests with scarlet surplices preceded the image of the Sainte-Vierge, a crude silver-plated statue borne between two poles on a faded rug, expressionless and shoddy. Carrying the poles two men dressed like boxers with towels round their necks sweated under their burden. Behind them a crowd of followers slouched along, nearly all women with priests among them, their responses drowned under gusts of singing higher up in the procession.

Along the edges, children ran imitating the only Latin words they knew, "*Dominum Nostrum Jesum Christum*" and at the cafés on the side the waiters went on serving Cinzano, the games of draughts and cards continuing without a head turned, while below the loud jazz came drifting up from the converging loudspeakers.

Within a few minutes the whole charade had practically collapsed, the singing disintegrated except for the solitary rallying cries of the priests, and the girls toiled up the hill shamefaced and meaningless. It was like some ghastly amateur play that had unaccountably misfired before a local audience; somewhere, one felt, from the sidestreets a sandwichboard man would materialise, bearing a great printed placard with the words "God is not mocked" in bold type all over it.

ALL THE bus services were run by private individuals, usually without offices, so it was extremely difficult to find out any sort of time-table or arrange plans. The buses left more or less at the whim of the owner, who was also the driver on the shorter routes, coming in from the villages, picking up mail and supplies, and then going out again.

The bus to Nonza arrived at nine and left at half-past twelve. By the time it was ready to leave it had been filled up inside about three-quarters full with wicker covered stone and glass jars of *pastis*, white and red wines. On the roof were bags of potatoes, vegetables, and a coffin; on the back had been tied suitcases, a bicycle, more parcels, and boxes of gaseous fruit juice.

There were only a dozen or so passengers; a great burly peasant, old and evil, like the film convict of *Great Expectations*, a number of women sitting with shopping bags piled up on their laps, an engaged couple from Canelle, a village some way out, a pregnant girl with peroxide hair, and the two sons of the driver, dark, handsome boys, who spoke a smattering of American slang-talk English, and wore jazzy socks with suede shoes.

The start was delayed half an hour by a puncture which, almost for certain, meant missing lunch at the other end—though the journey was only thirty kilometres it took two hours, owing to the natural slowness of the bus and the detours in the steep mountain roads.

The weather had grown very hot—a damp, sticky heat without much sun, and the inside of the bus sweated through the lacquer of flies that coated the cracked glass windows.

The road at once climbed straight above Bastia, circling and re-circling over it till the top of the gradient was reached, and the sea lay behind in a smooth grey paste with the sunk ship sitting up like a model in a bath. The coast-road down the east side tapered away by strips of bared sand, along swamps with rushes standing out in tiny head-dresses over still, stagnant pools of water.

Then the bus turned away into the hills, the banks of the road clouded with orange ferns and *maquis* reaching right up to where the bare rock of the mountains began. The road snaked between high overhanging boulders, ancient wizened faces screwed up into the slate patterns of stone, and the white strip of the route, wriggling like a dry river bed edging a valley down to the sea.

Towards Patrimonio the landscape quietened, like a change in the conversation, and vineyards, squared out into suburban allotments, stretched up to where the hills began again.

With the wet heat a little purer because of the height, and clouds breaking in soft showers on the mountains, the perfumed smell of the *maquis* became sharp and edged. The rain took off the weight of dust, a bridal purity of scent breaking over the road. A feeling of relief, like the passing of a nervous crisis, spread itself over the afternoon.

The sea emerged in its usual way, suddenly round a bend, with its bland air of having been there all the time, blue and deep with feathers of white round the rocks, and the northern capes hooded with mist. There was not a boat on the water, but seagulls fluttered out from miniature cathedrals in the rock and fanned their wings hopelessly from side to side, before landing again on ridges lower down.

Clusters of houses appeared propped up on the hills overlooking narrow inlets, each group marked on the map, the bigger ones, with twenty or thirty cottages and a church, in bolder lettering like cities.

Farinole, Negro, and then Nonza, built up in ledges over the rockface, with the rotting shell of the Martello Tower perched over the sea, in which Casella had held out single-handed against a Genoese attack in force, by firing his musket from each window of the Tower in turn and simulating a garrison.

But nothing remained of his gesture in the faces of old men and women sitting about on the rock ledges, staring out round them in the dull afternoon, with everything closed—the church, the school, the gendarmerie—and nowhere to stay, no food, for the bread hadn't come, and only Albo seven kilometres away round the headland as a possible place for the night.

By the time the old woman had pushed back the beaded curtains under her "*Pension en Famille*" notice and said there was no room anywhere, the bus was already out of sight.

Great rain clouds burst over the hill, black galleons in full sail shaking out huge drops over the dust in the roadway.

There was nothing for it but to take up the bags and walk on, sheltering under a rock when the storm was at its worst, and finishing up a melon and bottle of wine which was all there was left for lunch. Dotted all round were the white sepulchres of the cemetery guarding their dead under domed roofs, and iron railings glistening in the rain-wash amongst dark cypresses.

Afterwards the sun came out, with swallow-tails flying out of the scrub and cicadas singing above the tongues of sand, where the sea came in on cellophane curlers, hardly unrolling itself from its green basin.

.   .   .   .   .

Faintly, like an undercurrent through telephone wires, then louder, dance music started coming up from under the headland. A gramophone seemed to be playing in the middle of the rock, some secret transmitting station someone had forgotten to turn off.

Then below the road, perched over rocks at the side of a small bay, four or five red-roofed houses straggled on either side of a pathway. In the middle of them two semi-cubist villas, pink with pale blue windows, fanned out like a half-planned seaside resort that had never been completed.

From the larger of these the music was coming, and dimly inside, through wedges of people blocking all the entrances, couples could be seen clogged together, moving slowly round in a sultry tango.

A few ramshackle cars lay outside what appeared to be a hotel, and for a moment it seemed like an oasis which might disappear at any second.

But the hotel was real and though there were no rooms left—it was the Fête de Saint Roc—there were spare mattresses and a shed outside, next to the terrace which was used during the day as a restaurant.

The *patron*, a little bright fellow like a ventriloquist's dummy with blue overalls and a wooden leg, came hopping out of a cellar with his wife and said Yes, Yes, they would willingly prepare a bed in the restaurant at night and they were very sorry there were no rooms, but, you know, the Fête. . . .

As if to bear out their words, the bell from a small stone building near the shore started ringing and the gramophone started up again competing against the stern notes of the bell, the shuffle of dancers' feet like leaves piling up and swishing down over the simple chapel.

Outside the door a priest pulled the corded rope of the bell, wearily, like a commissionaire outside a not too successful theatre who senses the draw of the attraction across the road, but knows himself unable to do anything about it.

A few women came out of the houses, old, creased figures like paintings, shawls over their heads, picking their way down singly into the chapel with the lights burning on the altar and the sun beating down

100

NONZA

outside. Then a young girl in a white blouse and red pleated skirt, her dark hair running out from under a coloured scarf tied over her head, led down a blind, hunched-up man, his stick tapping out like uncertain morse on the rocks.

The dancing above stopped for a few moments and when nobody came out, the priest gave up ringing the bell and went inside amongst the flickering candles and immobile dark shapes waiting for some sort of communication.

All the next hour, in between the dancing and the gusts of music, the sad intoning voice could be heard at Mass, while on the terraces opposite, trays of *pastis* were carried out at intervals to the sweating parties from the dance hall.

.   .   .   .   .

Though the sun had become hot outside, the sea flecked with a few bathers in the cleft between the headlands, the dancing continued without a stop from the early afternoon till two or three o'clock the next morning.

It was as though some fanatical rite was being enacted, some test of religious endurance, which demanded this monotonous circling shuffle in the packed room with the heat spilling down the girls' make-up and outside, the Promised Land of the sea waiting—something not to be tasted till the penance had been completed.

Up on the hill, a white cross amongst the vines that grew into each other from the two headlands, the village of Ogliastro looked down on the road that the great humps of grassless earth and rock clumsily pushed out round the cliffs. From up there, the few houses empty and shuttered with their occupants all at the Fête, Albo looked as if someone had taken up a hundred yards of the boarding on the front at Southend and planked them down amongst these mountains, with a dance hall to bring in a quick return. But somehow the money hadn't lasted, and before the pin-tables and sideshows could arrive, the proprietor had made off, leaving the pink turrets and brick red roofs, the old table gramophone and scratched records as a bad debt.

Before dusk a procession of children followed the priest, holding up a Cross, round the chapel path and up along the cliff edge, where in a cove fishing boats lay amongst the rocks, their brown nets spread out with the smell of seaweed and salt breaking out of them.

More buses began to arrive from all along the coast, Canari, Marinca, Scala, while tables were laid out on the terrace with paper tablecloths and bottles of wine. Parties came down from the dancing, baskets of food with them, and sat down at the water's edge to eat. The sea had grown motionless and sitting outlined in the dark the rows of people seemed more than ever like refugees waiting for a boat to some unknown future.

From the hotel building, bowls of steaming *bouillabaisse* were brought out to the terrace, then langouste and stuffed tomatoes, pears, and figs from the trees overhanging the road, soft and with red melting chalices.

The tables filled up, more and more wine was brought, the men sat in white shirtsleeves, the women in cheap cotton frocks, like a charabanc excursion party, while the daughter and son from the hotel rushed out in relays from the kitchen, and the hoarse music drifted down over the Children of Israel, "A Little on the Lonely Side", "I Can't Give you Anything but Love, Baby", "Jealousy", their anaesthetic increased by the remorseless nostalgia of the French recordings.

The party began to get a little drunk, clapping on the tables like rooters at an American football game, and singing. In the middle a thin, sallow young man with a beautiful light tenor voice sang some nostalgic love-song for a few minutes and the talking stopped. But when he had finished, the waves of louder voices broke over a woman

103

who had begun to sing in a tenuous contralto, the chairs scraped backwards and forwards, the crowd on the beach gave up their vigil by the Galilean sea, and the mob with arms round each other swayed up to the Casino glittering in the night.

In the bay a solitary fishing boat was out, its lamp glowing over the water and its nets draining out in the slide of light.

The noise up the hill went on almost till dawn. Next door all the babies were laid out on mattresses, like parcels in a cloak-room waiting to be collected.

The narrow road to Ogliastro ran up the steep ravine between the two headlands. The houses, cream, pale green, pink, propped themselves up round a miniature church, no bigger from the bay than children's bricks. In the ravine a dark multi-coloured strip of vegetation, like the hair down a man's stomach, exaggerated the bare scrub on either side, marked only with the white ribbon of the road and the pylons that disappeared over the hill.

A signpost, almost withered away like a paralysed arm, pointed the way up the path, with the village itself hidden by the thread of the hill. Glittering in the sun the white rounded domes of family tombs—"La Famille Peleschi 1932", "Famille Longo 1919"—with effigies of the Virgin wreathed in rusty ferns faced one another in eternal complacency. Over the smooth surfaces lizards with purple and light green skins skidded like racing cars.

Further up, vines lay in fields of leaf on the higher side of the hill; on the other, fig trees hung over the loose wall, the pale yellow fruit hanging in ear-rings down from the thin branches. From the ravine, streams of water poured down amongst exotic broad-leaved plants, the ferns splaying out under over-hanging rocks, inset like the expensive garden ornamentation of a night-club—with, instead of orchids, white bell-shaped flowers stretching pale necks into the water, and dark green lichen and cress closing over them.

Behind the fig-trees, peaches, hanging like coloured lamps on a Christmas tree, lolled unreal and indolently golden with smudges of rouge emerging under the chaperoning leaves. Across the rough-stoned path, heavy, kimono'd butterflies, orange and russet, flopped from wall to branch. Through everything the submerged silver of the waterfall glistened like a thermometer.

At the top, under the distant velvet skyline, the cross of the village was pinned like a butterfly drugged on its setting board. There was no one in the streets; the windows of the houses were all barred; the church was shut.

104

It was as though constant living so close to this isolated profusion of plant and perfume, fruit and water, had been too much of an excess for the population, and yearly for the good of their souls they left their homes.

All round on the mountains the slopes were bare and stony. Half-way down the ravine the waterfall ran out.

ST. FLORENT

ALBO HAD been away from history, away from the meaningless political slogans, away from shops, advertisements, refuse.

St. Florent straggled down from a disused fortress on a cliff, a road of newer houses, square and night-dress pink, added onto the crumpling village that overhung the quay.

At the point where the two joined a war memorial stood encircled by trees. Round this the road forked westwards across the back of the bay, along a marsh that dried out into the Desert des Agriates, and beyond that to the sea again.

The other turning dribbled away into the narrow cobbles of the port, slanting up over the sea walls, with cave-like houses opening in black holes onto the burnt white of the street. From the harbour the smell of drains drifted up and lay in the air; below, on the dark scum of water, the emptyings of refuse pails floated about in oily splashes of colour, innumerable moving contours of garishly made-up negresses forming and dissolving themselves in the dingy kaleidoscope.

The newer houses appeared to edge away from the harbour, like prim girls averting their eyes from the ruins of history, telling themselves that nothing else could be expected after all these years of lost battles, with the great Dubonnet advertisement staring out in moralising letters from its mauve background on their walls and the bougainvillea drenching the neat squat gardens in heavy gusts of perfume.

Round the square were a few shops—a newsagent's with *L'Humanité*, picture-postcards and the *Continental Daily Mail* days old pinned up in a rack, a grocers, a café, and a garage. On the pavement an old woman sat in a small circle of tomatoes, with flies in a thick screen over the fruit, pitilessly eating their way towards her so that in a few hours they would be converging on her actual body, infiltrating through the thin black folds of her draperies.

But there was no fruit in the shops, though all along the hillsides the vines were heavy with grapes and the figs pulled the branches to the ground. They had their expensive markets waiting in Cannes, Marseilles, Paris, London, and there were none over for the villagers

106

ST. FLORENT—THE HARBOUR

except the scrawny throw-outs and the over-ripe melons sent in daily from Bastia.

The few fishing boats had already come in and on the quay in patches of shade boys desultorily mended nets, stretching them out to dry on the hot slabs of the jetty.

A group of tourists from Paris in bright, contrasting clothes slashed through the drab black of the women sitting outside their doorways. Girls moved about in the square with baskets over their heads or stood round the water taps filling jugs. The church lay out of sight, hidden behind the row of shops. The flies remorselessly drilled their way through the heap of tomatoes.

.   .   .   .   .

At lunch in the Hotel de l'Europe overlooking the harbour, with the heavy bead curtains rattling and the mosquitoes climbing up outside the netting windows, beautiful Patrimonio wine, golden and tasting like sherry, was brought in by the owner of the vineyard. Lobsters lay across the table on green plates, and afterwards there were miniature cutlets with haricot beans, peaches, black figs and grapes on a blue tablecloth.

Outside the heat had driven everybody off the streets.

.   .   .   .   .

The beaches stretching along away from the port lay under the dead eye of the fortress. There was no sand but long strips of brown gravel, with pale green and polished white pebbles toning in with the larger red stones.

The shore was empty. All round the bay hills rose up cutting off the sky and the sun splintered over the blue water that fell back in ennui off the shingle.

In the evening an English yacht came in and anchored in the harbour. A boat was put in and search made for a musician and a singer to go on board.

Interest rustled amongst the beaded curtains like a wind getting up. Faces peered out of the shutters. Musicians materialised on the quay, with guitars under their arms and accordions. A singer appeared, dark and Italian-looking, brandishing a few words of English as if they were talismans, repeating over and over again, "Spitfire—I fly Spitfire" and breaking into soft beautiful snatches of Manon.

The yacht belonged to a Colonel and his wife, who had about nine guests on board, and a crew of fifteen. They had sailed from

Southampton a fortnight earlier and had been to Oporto, Algeciras, and Gibraltar, calling in here for two days to get supplies before going on to Italy. Then they were returning to Cannes and flying back to England.

Some of the party on board were in evening dress; cocktails were produced out of silver shakers and tins of Three Castles cigarettes stood about on small tables.

The lights had come out in the port, the buildings timeless and beautiful across the water as if they were always used to being seen like this— with a man singing to a guitar from a yacht in the bay, with small boats drifting round like moths lured by the music, their oars folded up and men lying back in the dark.

After dinner there was dancing in Le Petit Caporal under an awning of leaves twined round netting with a gramophone churning out tangos.

The people from the yacht came out; the singer began again, silently drunk and a little overplaying his part, all the facile romanticism welling up in the expressive lyric voice, the hands saying this is how we really are, simple, beautiful, gay, while rows of dark-eyed children and young men smoking cigarettes crowded round the edges of the square stone floor, their eyes trailing behind the evening dresses swishing like faded butterflies in the pale light. And outside on the pavements the dirt lay about festering with flies ; children, with sores growing up under their dirt, tried to keep awake on the laps of young girls in black condemned to wear ceaseless mourning, and the embittered Communist farmer sat silently staring with faint contempt in his eyes.

The singing went on, the whole thing operatic and unreal, the characters stepping out of their normal lives into a world of romantic pretence, their gestures slightly awkward and wooden, like the gestures in a very old film.

Then, almost as if a new reel had been added, incongruous and misplaced, the whole atmosphere changed. There was a grunt from a group of men sitting on one of the walls, and a sullen-eyed figure, red-faced and unshaven, with strands of hair sweatily congealed across his nearly bald head, lurched over to where a solitary bulb hung in the awning, unscrewed it and while everyone was watching him but unaware of the implications, hurled it like an angry child on to the floor.

At once a commotion blew up, a great buzz of noise as though a door had been suddenly opened. The singer stopped in the middle of a gesture, as if the camera had stopped, freezing him into absurdity. Everyone stood up and crowded round the man who was staring at the singer, his hands half-clenched in red, unfinished-looking lumps, and the broken bulb, like a childhood obsession, smashed at his feet.

Then from out of the throng a little woman in black came rushing up between the two men, her arms wrapped round the man who had broken the bulb, imploring him, beseeching him to come away. As other men came up, he broke free, spat and lunged away out into the dark street.

Immediately, the singer, as if waking out of a hypnosis, started waving his hands about, protesting his innocence, saying "*J'étais matelot et je chantais, je chantais,*" as though his past too had to be explained away. But nobody was listening.

Collected in groups they were all discussing animatedly their private reactions—the imaginary director out of sight in the bushes calling out "More life, more life"—and the singer's broken heart melting away in his outstretched hands.

The slight apprehension amongst the women died away. The chairs were pushed forward again, the well-bred conversation smoothing away the *faux pas*. The *coup d'état* had failed, the Revolution for Independence had come to nothing.

The gramophone was put on loudly and people began dancing through the thinning crowd. The scene had been shot and now life had to go on.

Below the terrace, the riding lights of the yacht glittered discreetly over the harbour, the demure lines half-visible through the night. Among the dingy boats on the waterfront, which lapped up and down on the swelling surface, she seemed to be daintily reiterating the place of her birth.

.　　.　　.　　.　　.

In the early morning and by night the town was beautiful—the buildings fitted like models over the edge of the water, trees emerging in green oases through the stained wash-houses with pink running out over them from the sky.

In the darkness lights hung in the windows, miniature cathedrals with candles burning out the signals of endurance.

Then faces grew out of the shadows, cigarette ends glowed over the sea walls and the intangible voices died away in lost encounters.

But after a few days the spell breaks. The landscape, the sea, the buildings become part of a backcloth that is no longer noticed because there is no surprise left. It is time to go.

TRAIN JOURNEY

THE MICHELINE was full of smart tourists off the Nice boat, all on their way to Ile Rousse or Calvi.

It started off on time, the one punctuality that seemed to be taken seriously. The route was in a sharp "V", going down south nearly to Corte before turning up steeply to the north-west coast.

The whole of the railway was built through rock, so that it was like going along in a trench, with glimpses of wonderful towns inset into mountains and only a legendary reason for existence, hanging out of the sky round turns in the track.

Vescovato, Campile, Caravaggia and then down into the base of the "V" to Ponte-Lecchio, where the train stopped for a few minutes, and people rushed out for drinks from the station tap. There was panic for a few seconds when the train started off again with several passengers left behind. But unlike Lawrence's trains in Sardinia, it went back and picked them up.

There were two carriages, one more or less filled with peasants and a few campers, spectacled girls with great packs on the luggage racks above them, the other with sophisticated, heavy-jowled men, with women in three-quarter length trousers and Veronica Lake hair styles, very sunburnt and expensively simple.

In the corner a Dominican sat reading his Bible unconcernedly, his brown habit reaching out over a blue check shirt. Occasionally he looked out of the window through dark glasses and several pages blew over together, but he went on reading as if it was still at the same place, or as though it made no difference anyway, it was all the same hard message of love.

Alongside the railway the road twisted, always a ledge or two lower down, and the dry river-bed snaked through the maze of mountains and ravines.

On the hills odd flocks of goats stampeded away at the train's approach, shepherds in black trousers with red sashes sitting on the verges, miles from any human life.

The landscape became more unreal with the heat. It was harsh and isolated, not a part of natural existence, but something that had always been there, motionless and without sensation, since the beginning. It

112

ILE ROUSSE HARBOUR

had not been shaped for use, but simply existed as some sort of ruthless deposit that the sky touched into beauty but never moved.

Then small towns, like lost civilisations, identified themselves in splinters of light as the train circled them over and over, producing new facets in series of "still" photographs pasted on at every angle, Lama, Novella, Belgodere.

Then at Regino, a village with a few houses round the railway line, a girl in a red swagger coat, silk stockings and high-heel shoes, got off, and climbed into a waiting lorry that drove up into the hills.

The few peasants sitting on the platform amongst tiny, dirty children never moved or looked up. It seemed not unnatural, nor at any rate important. Life went on.

Gradually the sea came into sight, the headlands all round softened in an apricot, evening light. The railway dipped down and ran along sandbeaches lying like sables thrown onto the edge of the land.

A long jetty stretched into the sea, beyond rocks where a lighthouse built like a modern flat stood aloof, cool and functional, and behind it the waterside buildings of Ile Rousse sagged into dingy obscurity, fell away into groups of high plane trees and, as if revived, re-emerged into a new enormous hotel, smart villas, and trellised gardens.

.   .   .   .   .

Ile Rousse was founded by Pascal Paoli and had the best hotel in Corsica. The Hotel Napoléon Buonaparte dominated the whole town like a benevolent dictator.

114

ILE ROUSSE—CAFÉ DES PLATANES

It was at once very real and very symbolic—a symbol of striving like Kafka's Castle—that hardly anyone really attained, at least no one that anybody knew. The people who stayed there came from and went back to a different world.

When they arrived, a flag of their countries was flown beside the much larger flags of the Hotel Napoléon and France. Their identities were established so that everyone knew they were there.

The Hotel Napoléon Buonaparte had its own sector of the beach, surrounded with barbed wire. There were special tents, and striped parasols planted in the sand like rare flowers with red and white unfolding leaves.

There were other hotels, too, less ostentatious but respectable and expensive, only they had no chance against the Hotel Napoléon.

It stood right in the middle of the newer houses, its flags fluttering confidently over all the other buildings, well up over its own plane trees. High colonnades stood on either side of the entrance and over the doors at the end of the drive huge diamond studs glowed like jewels at night. Lawns lay under the terraces and at the back, tennis courts were laid out amongst flowers. When the lights came on at night it was as though Parliament was sitting. Inside, beautiful girls in flowing organdie dresses hung over the chromium rails of the American Bar. The barman was handsome, with fine features, silver hair, and that particular look of gauging all clients' individual incomes which the best barmen cultivate. The manager was like Peter Lorre, but more animal and distracted, lank hair hanging wetly over his wide forehead.

But the feeling inside the hotel was quite unreal. Somebody had by mistake directed everyone to the wrong place. These people sitting about in the lounges were in their imagination somewhere quite different. Certainly not on the same coast as Propriano or Porto Vecchio, where the streets were covered with human dung because there were no lavatories and where children wore the same clothes all the year round. This was not only a few dozen miles from where in the mountains the old men and women couldn't read or write, where there was no fresh water and where men settled their differences with guns because they were too personal for strangers to interfere with. This was another world altogether, a world where there were no politics because the hotel took care of all that, where there was no dirt because the hotel protected you from seeing it, where only your money was required as a passport.

The rest of the town was cowed by it. A few fishing boats lay by the quay, there were some shops in the narrow port streets, a big, beautiful

116

ILE ROUSSE

square full of plane trees, and above the town inset into the mountains the buildings of Monticello and Corbara hanging like birdcages. But everybody sat about in the shade of the plane trees or by the palm trees opposite the hotel looking wistfully in. They seemed all to be talking in whispers.

The place itself, though, was quietly beautiful, framed like a locket by the high hills with blue sea stretching up over soft flat sand and the old houses draped at sunset with orange, green, and pink fading over them into the harbour water.

The beach was lined at the back with trees which ran along the railway line, and the hills behind became purple with the sun falling over the skyline.

    ·   ·   ·   ·   ·

All day long, soft sand over the fingers, copper burnt out like miniature coinage, the footprints of other lives. On the sea floor the sun burning contours of flame, dividing up the opalescent green water like a map. Shells lie about, soft pieces of glassy green stone. Girls emerge from beach costumes, shaking themselves free into semi-nakedness, throwing off at one go the whole of civilisation and diving into the water before it can grow again.

The sun moves, dust coating the palm trees; children play under enormous straw bonnets looking like Mexicans; all day the sun burns and scrutinises.

At night, under the plane trees, music comes out from the Café des Platanes with its red and green coloured lights. Bands from Paris and London play over the wireless, "Long Ago and Far Away", "Loin de Toi", "Time on My Hands".

Small boys sit about seriously in the shadows, listening, as if some great story was being told. The lighthouse flashes in the harbour.

The soft melting songs spill over the warm, night air, a soothing antidote to unhappiness. Inland, a different, deadened civilisation is insulated by the mountains.

PÈRE OBEIN

THE SUN hung over the landscape like a bulb of heat that had been left on all night.

The road to Corbara was straight up into the mountains, a direct path that seemed to go into the sky till near the top it swung round the curve of the hill and approached the town from the other side.

From the sea upwards great clumps of cactus, with prickly pears the colour of peaches grouped on them in bunches, hung over the road. Above them, beyond where the cottages faded into scrub, fig trees leant over wooden railings like women straining to overhear conversations. Then further up in the interstices of rock, cyclamen and asphodels grew out of cracks in the stone.

An old man dressed in a black velvet coat and trousers, black felt hat, white shirt and scarlet sash, passed on a donkey on his way down hill, his rifle jogging up and down on his shoulder. Otherwise the morning was empty of movement except for white butterflies and the sea coming in silently below.

Drifts of heavy scent hung over the road, *maquis* and eucalyptus mixed together, aloes and palm trees. The sky and the sea were the same colour, the sun a disc burning away in its own rays.

After walking an hour, there was sea on both sides of the headland, strips of sand with a few houses lost amongst olives round the bays, and Algajola a flutter of white stone at the edge of emerald water.

Birds began to circle higher up, motionless in the blue desert as if hung on invisible wires. Then slowly they moved, black and ruthless, like revolutionaries, in concentric circles.

Vineyards in terraces ridged up between bald patches of rock, and alongside them peach trees, with a few men thinning the heavy branches, glowed against the trails of green.

Corbara spread itself over the apex of the hill, pale pink stains of houses in uneven rows under the rock, with the minaret of the church breaking into the sky and the crumbling castle falling away on either side of the saddle of rock.

The village was nearly deserted, as though its life had been sapped away by the sun. Two or three men sat under a chestnut tree and a woman in black filled a pitcher from the tap that spouted out of the

119

rock. But everyone else seemed to have gone, for nearly all the houses were shut up or in ruins, the windows plain holes of black as if they had been bored into.

Further up, past old bricked-up chapels built on jasper with orange trees foaming between sharp boulders, the road led up another mile bounded by walls smoothed out on the rock. Very near the top the white rectangle of the Dominican monastery, half-covered by olive trees, shimmered in the blue air.

It was imaginable, coming up to it, that here men could say, "This is the end of the search, the road does not go back but only onwards."

A path switched off the road to Santa Antonia up into the monastery itself. High walls with barred windows faced onto a terrace levelled over the rock; a façade like a battlement with its huge grey door bolted seemed to turn towards the mountain, away from life and the link of the sea miles below.

At the top the wind was blowing strongly, leaves sailing in the air from the chestnut trees and birds still hovering over the hillside, sometimes screaming down on to crags of rock.

Adjoining the bolted façade was a small chapel, grey and cool with a lamp glowing on the altar. Two or three rows of hard chairs were

stood up at the front and the rest of the space had been cleared away, with more chairs piled up on top of each other in the corners. All along the sides were small altars with figures carved in olive wood of the Sainte-Vierge and symbolic incidents on the Cross. But it was simple and good after the pink sugary decoration of the village churches, with their crude vulgarities and cheap brazen ornamentation.

There was no one inside. But at the end of the terrace next to it a faded green gate with "*Passage Réservé*" on it shut in a small cemetery with cypresses rising darkly over simple white tombstones. A few were legible, "*Soeur Thérèse* 1879–1940", "*Ici repose Thomas Antonio*", the letters fading under the shadows of the cypresses.

Outside the big grey door a wire bell hung down loosely. When it was rung its sound faded away like an echo diminishing down a hall of mirrors, endlessly into nothingness. But no reply came, and through the large rusted keyhole it was possible to see another grey door stretching up to the roof and on it a blistered white board marked "*CLOTURE*" with under it in smaller letters "*On ne visite pas*".

A narrow drive ran up below the terrace and up to another double-sided gate alongside the cemetery. High walls all along made it impossible to see in and the windows of the annexe were all barred up and shuttered.

The place seemed to be deserted, a little sinister in its air of facing into the rock, with the unseeing eyes of the windows barred as if to prevent anyone returning into the world of men.

The bell in the church tower struck half-past seven, though it was already after ten, its echo dying into a silence that seemed to say, "Time is not time in your sense here, but exists independently", the hands of the clock moving without reference to the world's time, like the slow unrelated talk of a lunatic.

The wind was blowing incessantly, dry and warm, vainly dropping away from the steep rock into ravines stretching sheer down, with the houses of Corbara white in the green hillside and the sea far below, blue and disconnected.

On the skyline the figure of a shepherd outlined itself against a rock, the echo of his voice calling his flock, coming down as though it was from an enormous distance, but clear and perfectly reproduced.

The leaves swished about in the wind, just turning yellow, and piled themselves up at the feet of the Saint Dominique statue at the bottom of the path.

The gaunt granite rocks jutted out all round, falling into a space urgent with suicide.

121

Then suddenly, when it seemed that the monastery had been shut up for the summer or had been deserted through a sudden break up of faith, a key rattled in the great, grey door, and a figure emerged, bracing itself against the noise of the wind-lashed sunlight.

.　　　.　　　.　　　.　　　.

Père Obein was a small, plumpish man with the face of a *bon viveur* half-disguised under a stubble of grey beard, pale blue eyes intensified by steel-rimmed glasses, and a deep throaty chuckle. He had been at Corbara over thirty years.

Waving his pale hands like frightened birds under the black and white folds of his habit, he said, "You must excuse me for being so long, but we very rarely get any visitors here and sometimes the wind rings the bell. There is always wind here, summer and winter, warm, dry winds from Algeria that get on the nerves and keep one indoors. But you must come inside and let me show you our retreat."

He led the way through the grey doors, across a passageway with rooms on either side and into the cloisters.

In the centre of the quadrangle the soft red mouths of geraniums and dark roses gathered up the sun off the white stone buildings.

The sinister, inhuman spirit that had seemed to hover in the wind outside was completely shut out. The wind was baulked amongst this quiet, friendly garden surrounded by stone pillars, with all round an air of seclusion and unobtrusive spirituality.

"It is nice here in the sun," Père Obein went on, slowly walking round the cloister, "a good place to return to. A lot of things have happened here, cruel, terrible things. You see that slot in the wall"—he pointed to an aperture barred up with three rusty cylinders—"that was a prison where defaulting priests were put. They slept on a stone floor and received Communion through the bars. But that was a rare thing. A long time ago," and he laughed throatily.

"But let us walk in the sun, and if it doesn't bore you I'll tell you the whole story." He shot out a sideways glance from behind his sun-blinded spectacles and went on:

"In 1430 Nicolas, Bishop of Tine in Croatia, who was born in Corbara Castle, decided to found an orphanage here. He realised the wonderful natural wealth of the countryside, the clear water in the mountains, the abundance of ground for fruit and flocks.

"So he laid the original foundations amongst these blocks of granite and started his orphanage. But about twenty years later, in 1456, Mariano de Muro, and Matteo d'Ocebiatana, who were fathers of an

122

order called the Obsevatins, visited the place and decided to enlarge it for use as a Franciscan monastery.

"They did this and the monastery became known as the Convent de Saint-François de la pïeve d'Aregno.

"But let me show you the chapel," Père Obein continued, "nearly all the great families in Corsica have representatives buried in the vaults there."

He pushed open a door which led into the chapel close to the altar. The lamp was still glowing and the place was still empty, but through the far door beyond the trees a deep blue ribbon of sea lay like a tapestry.

"The Franciscans built all this," the Father went on, pointing round, "the marble altar here, the sculptured pulpit, and all those hand-carved stalls in the vestry. They were skilled artists, very Italian by temperament, many by birth of course, and you can see that from all their decoration."

He dropped his hands. "Then the first crisis occurred in this monastery, the first of, I'm afraid, very many. After having been here for three hundred and thirty-five years, the Franciscans were expelled by the Revolutionary authorities in 1792."

Père Obein took off his glasses and wiped them with a piece of black velvet. The lines round his eyes increased, folds of weak flesh that seemed only to be pushed away by the determination of the pallid blue pupils.

"All the books in the Library, over a thousand of them, were destroyed. The buildings were sold as national property to a man called Louis Orticoni of Monticello who in turn sold them to the town of Corbara.

"By 1857 there was nothing left of the cloisters but ruins. The gardens had been sold off in separate lots. In fact only the church was kept up and that simply because so many local families were buried there.

"You'll notice there is only a single stained glass window," Père Obein continued, replacing his glasses and genuflecting as he stepped behind the altar, "but it represents the meeting of St. Francis and St. Dominique—you can see them greeting and embracing one another."

Over his head the pale effeminate faces were pressed to each other, red and green glass forming a religious sunset behind the white faces and the legs pressed forward straining their exaggerated calf muscles above the altar.

"But in 1857, by a lucky chance, two *Frères Prêcheurs*, Father Bourard and Father Besson, spotted the ideal situation and possibilities of the ruins and obtained the consent of the town of Corbara to reconstruct the monastery.

"They were granted this and permission was obtained to open a school, which Father Bourard presided over as Prior for four years."

The hands fluttered nervously amongst the robes, lost children searching for a crucifix to hold onto. Then the voice went on. "But he died a few years later, a martyr, shot by the Paris Communards.

"Before this though, the French Dominicans had been replaced by Italians who had been expelled from their provinces—amongst them de Bonifacio and Vannutelli, who became Cardinals, and Didon, the famous preacher who was sent here for expressing too liberal opinions in Paris."

A light broke through the pale eyes. "He wrote wonderful letters, you know, about the view from this chapel. He used to love sitting out in winter early in the morning and looking down at the sea. '*Le soleil darde avec force ses beaux rayons, le vent secoue rudement son aile, la mer a ces reflects d'acier. Sa grâce toute bleue semble protégée par une cuirasse mètallique*'."

He pointed down at steel rivets plunged into the stone floor of the chapel. "The hobnails of the soldiers rubbed away the marble and

weakened the supports. Under this is only a sort of shifting subsoil, different from the granite in the cloisters."

In an altar on the side a wooden Sainte-Vierge had been carved out of the roots of an olive tree—the shape of the root remained, contorting the whole base of the figure into an agonised tension of muscle. Above it a Christ looked pityingly, but helplessly, down at where a German soldier had gashed the face of the Virgin and a white scar bit into the wood as though an acid tear had congealed.

"The Italians left about 1884 and returned to their provinces. The Noviciat Français took over, but a few years later a second great break in our history occurred.

"A law against brotherhoods was passed in 1903 and the nine monks who were here at the time were expelled. They were forced to sell all the property of the convent for practically nothing and according to the original lease the contents of the church reverted to the parish of Corbara. But the buildings again fell into decay and ruin.

"During the Great War," Père Obein went on, his voice as certain as if he was reading out from his memory something he himself had written, "they brought German civilian prisoners of war here. They were put in the monks' cells and here, where I'm standing now"— he rubbed his thin fingers over the red, mapped marble—"they made a dormitory for their guards. The vestry and the church itself were stripped of everything and the flagstones and walls were rubbed of their inscriptions."

The sun was beating down on the red flowers beyond the cloisters as he opened the door and let a shaft of light in.

"It's not a very nice story," he said dispassionately, "but come, let us see something more cheerful." He shuffled out into the sun-whitened cloisters and waved his hand at a young monk who was coming across to the chapel from the far side.

"He's been away for three months, preaching in all the little mountain villages. There are not many educated priests left now, and we have to go out touring almost the whole time."

As if guessing a question he went on, "Yes, it is difficult for us. Only the very young have any interest. Then when they grow up, like everybody else they go away to France. We are left with a few children and old people who are worn out with nothing to do but drink. You have noticed, surely, the abandoned look of all the villages ?

"They are shut-up and empty with no one in the houses; the fields are half untilled; the vine terraces are left to get grown over through neglect. The only Corsica that lives is in France, split up in hundreds

125

of separate people—in Marseilles, in Lyons, in Paris. They only come back here to die."

He opened a door into a panelled room like an Oxford College hall. A few places were laid on simple white tables and in front of each place stood a bottle of wine and a bowl of figs.

"We live very simply but sufficiently here. Everything we eat is our own produce—vegetables and fruit from the gardens, our own wine, cows and sheep on the hills."

He pointed to a lectern built out from the middle of one of the walls. "Each day during meals we have a reading from the Bible; otherwise we keep silence."

An old tottering figure, with a huge polished head, came muttering into the refectory, a bowl of milk soup clutched in its shaking hands. Père Obein ignored him. "He's ninety-three," he said, with a change of voice, "and a bit out of his mind,"—and went on talking while the old man sucked at his soup muttering all the time to himself.

"We have four nuns here, who do all the cooking, washing and cleaning. They live in a wing by themselves and spend the whole day in work."

The hatch opposite lifted for a second and a white, spectacled face peered out from under its hood. Then like a veil the hatch dropped down.

The Father stepped out into the sun again, holding out his hands with the palms upturned to the heat. Huge black birds still circled overhead and the wind was blowing like a sea against the trees outside.

On the other side of the flowers a door was already open. "This is our common room," he said, "where we come after meals and read or listen to the news."

A small wireless stood in a corner by a glass-covered bookcase. In the middle of the room was a polished round table, with five leather armchairs pushed out from it.

On the table were files of newspapers and magazines—three or four copies of *La Croix*, and *La Vie*; a current number of *La Vie Intellectuelle* and *Lettres Françaises*; a few Paris dailies.

"Next door," Père Obein went on, "is the room where we hold our philosophical discussions. I would show it to you, only for a few days we have novices studying here and they work in there under a teacher."

He half-opened the door adjoining and a murmur of voices came through before he closed it again.

"Now I will show you where all our Rosaries are made." Further along, the quadrangle opened out into the garden and in the archway a door was let into the wall.

Père Obein pushed it open and, inside, sitting behind a huge desk was an elderly woman in a blue overall. She got up at once and came forward eagerly, her overall pockets bulging with rosaries.

Mlle X—Père Obein never introduced her but stood aloof outside after she had come forward—had been there for six years. Her brother had been one of the original pilots on the Paris-London air route. But in 1940 he had been shot down. After that she had decided to get away from life.

All the time she talked about him her eyes had a wild fanatical look and she pulled nervously and continuously at the jingling rosaries in her pocket. In a few moments she had told his whole life story, her mouth panting in spasms of weakness and showing gapped, bad teeth. Then she drew in her breath again and started repeating bits of the story, as if she needed approval and justification and praise—her eyes darting wildly about like trapped birds.

But Père Obein smiled her away and said, "We will go to the cellar and I will give you a drink of our wine before you go down. You must be thirsty."

He led the way out, the warm wind brushing back the vines on the terraces outside and falling away like waves against a breakwater, on the high cloister walls.

The cellar was cold and quiet as a cathedral. Père Obein put on a light, revealing a long stone passageway lined with barrels on either side. At the far end was a small annexe with spaces for bottles and a black wine press reaching nearly up to the stone roof. Hundreds of bottles protruded from the honeycomb of boxes.

"We make all our own wine," Père Obein said, taking down a bottle, "more than we can drink ourselves," his eyes lighting again like pale dragonflies and chuckling, bubbles breaking in the throat, "so we sell a lot of this to various merchants."

He poured out the wine into amber, fluted glasses. It was of a pure, cold strength, the taste unspoilt by any sort of processing and slightly raw.

"There are only twelve of us here at the moment, so you see we are well provided for. Nearly always there are four or five away preaching and then they come back here for a little while—to study and to prepare themselves, it is so very quiet here—and to discuss the various problems that have arisen. You see this is the only retreat we have in the island."

The hands made gestures, touching the barrels, the press, the big stone vats, demonstrations in parenthesis, as he went on, his voice human and experienced, in the dripping cool of the semi-darkness.

127

"But I will finish my story. Shortly after the Great War ended, a rumour spread round that a society was trying to lease the convent to make it into an Institution. But the villagers apparently wanted us." The eyes splintered behind the thick lens, "and they got in touch with the Order again, offering the buildings back.

"Everything was in ruin and in a state of vandalism. But it was decided to make the necessary repairs. We came back one by one, and now, you see, I have been here another 20 years."

Out in the sunlight again the leaves sailed about in whirlpools. The chapel bell was ringing, the sounds coming through the wind as if it were fog—clear and then disappearing, wrapped up in the noise of air.

Père Obein held out his hands. "Now I must leave you. Next time you come give me some warning and I can arrange food and a room for you. You must excuse my discourtesy in not being able to offer you more hospitality—but you know, with all the novices today, it is difficult for them in the kitchen."

The white hands rustled under the black and white habit, the folds of the cloth billowing out in sails as the wind bowled up against the plump figure. The convent seemed to be riding the mountain wind, like a galleon in the trough of steep waves.

Père Obein closed the big grey door behind him, the chapel bell still ringing out like a ship's bell. The buildings no longer looked sinister, but secure and human. The inhumanity, the turning back on life, had not existed. Instead there was this spiritual, cloistered oasis of learning, a place to gather wisdom and strength before going back into life.

CALVI

It was twenty miles down the coast to Calvi. Somewhere on the route an invisible frontier is crossed—the frontier between unhappiness and pleasure, between an oppressive past and between history that has been eased of pain.

Calvi is really not Corsica at all, but a part of the Côte d'Azur that has drifted away from its moorings. The ennui, the bitterness, the sense of abandonment that hangs over the rest of the island has been smoothed away by the Mediterranean—by a piece of sea that is sailed only for pleasure.

The huge fortress built onto rock rises up square and gaunt over the town—a flutter of red and white buildings separated from the quayside by palm trees. Behind, like a spine, a road runs up to the derelict naval prison that was reserved for the worst criminals and beyond that, over soft hills of *maquis*, mountains cut off the distance which gets piled up with clouds unable to cross.

The quaysides fall away into rocks on one side and on the other into long strips of white sand bordered by pine trees—the hills on the far side crowding in when the weather is bad, dark and purple like Scotland.

Calvi was the most faithful Genoese stronghold. On the gates of the citadel the words "*Civitas Calvi Semper Fidelis*" stand out as though they were written up yesterday—amongst the derelict garrison buildings shelled into surrender by Hood a hundred and fifty years ago.

All round the fortress gutted relics of different wars lay about—a rusted mortar, a still oiled ack-ack gun, emptied food tins, scrawled slogans.

Nearly all the castle buildings were ruined, staring blindly out at the blue sea through windowless slots, acre after acre overgrown, with the sun burning off the white cobbled paths and a deserted silence, like a pall of smoke, issuing out of the fissures in the brick.

Below, the sea was flecked with sailing boats, the blue water changing into bars of different colour, black over seaweed, emerald, pale cobalt —till it frilled over the dun sand, lost where the pines stood up like a green hairbrush, and the heads of bathers were olives thrown into the waves.

. . . . .

In the morning the fishing boats were the colour of washed shirts—
" *Roger et Henri* ", " *Angèle* ", " *Michèle* ", the names fading like rain on
newsprint—and figures draped over the sea walls as if posing. Everything was much cleaner here, the faintly tropical atmosphere rinsed
of its dirt, the cafés brightly painted, with fishermen in blue dungarees
leaning against murals like scenes in a smart revue.

Lapping against the breakwater the yachts from Cannes, sails spread
out to dry on the hot quay, the linen twisted up in agony, drained
out the sea in a tourniquet of sun.

These are the arteries that feed Calvi—the boats that put out at night
with oil, cocaine, heroin, langoustes.

Up in the hills, glittering like a castle, are the buildings of Calenzana
—they call it the village of gangsters.

At night in the Bar Américain the regulars arrive—the Comte M. de
B, with his garden of pink lilies, his aesthetic Catholicism, and two
years in Buchenwald. Apart from those two years, he has been here
every summer for twenty years, torn between hate and love—love
for the dark faces, the guitars at night, the *lamentos*, the savage landscape
with its sudden tendernesses: hate for the pimps, the roguery, the
brutality, the *ennui*.

130

CALVI—THE CITADEL

"Corsica is an abandoned island," he says, "but one where the pomp, the glamour, the excuses die hard. When Yusipoff was here with his suite, Oh the wonderful women, the great Russian orgies, the Cossacks, the drink—you should have seen the parties in the Archbishop's palace." He has a Clifton Webb voice, pale blue eyes, and hands like butterflies, suddenly made aware by Buchenwald of a new reality, so that all the past seems like a marine flower, a Dali painting, washed up, beautiful and dead. "But you must meet Keripoff, he lives there now you know. A most beautiful Englishwoman gave him the house in the Citadel and now it's a night club."

Drinking at the bar were a Paris interior decorator, an English dramatist, a young man from Air France, and the owner, a Dutch woman talking about Noel Coward, "He's so witty, you know."

The walk up to Keripoff's. The citadel buildings lemon sheets of stone in the moonlight, the narrow alleys opening into courtyards of silence, with sudden spaces, remote lovely perspectives seen under archways. The lighthouse beam swivels over the water, dying out on the headlands.

Then the solid stone house amongst empty barracks. Down a flight of stairs with Russian murals of Cossacks and Moujiks and into a drab room of faded splendour. Some *nouveau-riche* French tourists dance to a gramophone.

132

CALVI—VIEW FROM CITADEL

Keripoff himself was a burly, pale, Caucasian chief, with strong squat fingers, a fine head, and behind a bar his Corsican wife, changing the records. Keripoff pours out large Eau de Vies, "You must have this with me," he says, "*c'est la tradition de la maison*."

He goes back to look after the French tourists, now giggling a little, demanding "*le swing*". Fat women in striped dresses, with men in loose white coats, wearing thick glasses, their white flesh all red with sunburn.

The room looks suddenly dead. "*Mais tout reviendra*," Keripoff says as if in apology, "*doucement*." But never that world, the Caucasian dances, the toasts to the Czar, the orgies into the dawn. It is all as dead as the faded figures in the tapestries, lifelessly pinioned in their glass prisons.

.   .   .   .   .

They say that Nelson lost his eye during the bombardment of Calvi and that the piece of roundshot that did it still exists. They say too that Columbus was born there and there is a small plaque on a dingy little house near the citadel that commemorates his birth. But the Genoese claimed he was born in Genoa, and are supposed to have destroyed the record of his birth in Calvi from all the original documents.

Anyway, there is no feeling of history left in Calvi. The citadel area is a deserted village, its buildings gaping like blank pages with nothing more to say. Life has slowly dribbled away down the walls into the harbour and from there to the beach, the Grand Hotel and the American Bar.

Now it is simply a place to be happy in—away from the brooding interior, the filthy towns, the political agitators, the sense of doom. A place where at night, in an open-air café called the Bel Endroit, when the *tangos* and *paso dobles* have finished, you can hear the native Corsican songs, sung by fishermen to the accompaniment of guitars— soft, tragic laments of love and lonely decorations of death.

ST. FLORENT—PORTRAIT OF A BOY

THE BLACK MARKET RUN

AT Essitac, the transport agency in Ajaccio, they said there was a bus to Porto every day of the week except the next day. There was however one leaving in half an hour's time.

It was just possible to make it—to get back, pay the hotel, pack and rush up to the Grandval. But the bus was already full, people standing inside and sitting on top, and it would have been impossible to squeeze even a child through the doors.

Behind the bus there was a lorry being loaded with boxes. "You can sit on top if you like," the driver said; he was a man with a ferrety face, wooden leg and cloth cap. "I'll take you to Porto for four hundred francs. Be here at four o'clock."

By four o'clock a matelot going to Piana on leave, an art historian from the Beaux Arts at Besançon, a doctor and his wife on holiday, had all arrived and were placed on top of the boxes. The sky was still very threatening, and it looked as though it might start raining again.

The journey to Porto, the driver said, would take four hours. Actually it took five; a drive up through steep gorges into the mountains and then down again along the deeply indented coast with the sea a dark purple and the hills leaning over black and menacing. Small strips of beach, deserted and with no houses anywhere near, washed themselves up out of inlets into banks of light green canes waving on the edge of the shore. Then the road turned back into the mountains, high up over the Chioni valley, with no signs of cultivation and only sparse clumps of *maquis* covering the muzzled rocks.

It began to grow dark. The lorry headlights were switched on, picking out fantastic shapes in the rock as they swung round bends or fell into nothingness over narrow walled-in ledges. Then, after what seemed hours, with a cold misty rain blowing off the sea and the stars banked out under smudges of cloud, the lights of Piana glittered over a rise in the road—a slant of houses with feathery angles of light ricocheting off trees and mosquitoes caught in the headlamps, flying round in circles.

At the approach to the town a lorry lay across the road, already unloading into a warehouse. All the other occupants got off as the driver of the parked lorry turned down a small side-track—the doctor

and his wife, the sailor, and the art historian, fading away to houses
and to hotels shining under the rain.

Then the lorry went down into the main square and parked by
a shed under a chestnut tree. The boxes on top were taken off and
with a great deal of furtive stealth sacks of flour were pulled out from
underneath.

It became obvious that this was a regular black market run—done
at night on the days after boats had come in from Algiers. Besides the
flour there were numerous other smaller parcels bundled out under
canvas protections into the shed.

Three or four young men emerged out of the trees to supervise the
unloading—cigarettes stuck down onto lower lips, cloth caps pulled
over their faces, hands sullenly stuck into pockets.

No one spoke at all. The lorry driver kept on saying "Five minutes,"
as if to explain it all away and looking at his watch, while his assistant
pulled out the heavy bags and waited for the man in the shed to come
back from carrying the previous sacks.

Meanwhile the young men slowly gyrated in the thin rain, like
film extras waiting for the main character, unconcerned and un-
compromised. An imbecile tottered over from a café, his balance
so distorted he could hardly stand up, and stood by the truck, grinning
through protruding gapped teeth, while his eyes registered nothing at
all and his limbs shook continuously in a kind of interrupted St.
Vitus' dance.

Gradually the flour was all emptied out and the young men hung round the shed, while the bags were counted and a padlock was fastened on the door by the light of a torch.

Then the lorry lurched into gear and down the hill, past the blanched walls of the uncomprehending church, with its tower just striking nine and along under the shadow of dark, serrated rocks.

After about twenty minutes a few lights appeared out of the darkness. The lorry drew up by a bridge where there was a small hotel hanging over the river bank, amongst eucalyptus woods heavy with mosquitoes and with the sound of a waterfall spilling itself out from the pines above the bridge. "Porto," the driver said laconically, putting out one hand for the money and already letting off the brake with the other.

. . . . .

The hotel was a small shack, owned by a handsome Corsican who had fought with the British in the last war. The battle names were his touchstones of reality—the Marne, Passchendaele, the Somme—all through dinner he spoke of them with a sort of loving nostalgia, his d'Annunzio eyes softly eloquent and his white waved hair shining under the lamplight. A little girl, his granddaughter, brought in the food—hot soup, langoustes, cheese and wine—while in the background, like the great mountain symbol of F6, sat the old woman who must have been his mother, silent, omniscient, female.

All night the sound of the waterfall pressed into sleep, like an insistent foaming caress—the waves of the sea, the strong smell of eucalyptus, the divinity of the old woman nodding her head, all mixed up together. Continuous rivers of perspiration poured from us in the hot, wet atmosphere. But it turned cold towards dawn, with the huge, lined rocks of the Calanches falling out of the hands of the darkness.

. . . . .

The weather was better the next day—the sun came out over two pink and green marzipan hills, with a delta of dark green eucalyptus gathered up between them.

The waterfall broadened out into a river that forked round the wood and came out stagnant the other side. At the bottom a beach sloped down steeply into the sea, with crags of salmon rock shivering in the motionless pools. High up, inland, jagged peaks coated all the way with scrub unrolled right down to the sea.

There were only about ten houses in the village, three of which were hotels—the others were fishermen's or shepherds' cottages, clustered

PORTO—HOTEL BEDROOM

together halfway between the waterfall and the beach amongst fallen eucalyptus trees, vineyards, and a quarry.

In patches of shade donkeys moved restlessly as flies settled on their backs; round their delicate feminine legs chains hung, tying them together so they were able to move only very slowly. Huge butterflies flew in and out of the trees, Purple Emperors and White Admirals.

The beach was practically empty all day. In a solitary café overlooking the sea a boy and girl danced the whole burning afternoon to a tinny gramophone.

CARGÉSÉ

WHITE square houses in symmetrical, rectangular patterns; chestnuts foaming up over corners of roofs; the blue sky cloudless over the two headlands with the town like an amphitheatre between them.

At the foot of the bay the sea comes in to a small beach with a chestnut tree flowering out over the sand; boats lie in its shadow, fishermen coiling lobster pots on the rocks.

All up the hill cactus plants glow with fruit. A few olive trees are dark lines under the eyes of the white windows.

Over the bay, built onto two terraces, the Greek and Catholic churches face one another like stone boxers. In their shadows men lie stretched out, red sashes over pale blue trousers.

The flies circle mercilessly round the donkeys tied to the shade.

The houses are built at right angles, sloping down in terraces, with the hill disappearing under them as though it was tucked in—so looking out of the windows there is blue sea coming right up to the olive trees.

Behind the Catholic church the town crumbles away; a fig tree grows out of a gutted, roofless building. Then, beyond, the hills move in green waves, carrying life away out of sight.

The dark women lay out their washing under the orange trees.

.   .   .   .   .

Cargésé was founded in 1774 as a colony for the Greek exiles who had fled from the Turks and been granted a refuge by the Genoese.

About seven hundred had arrived in Corsica in 1676, after a treaty had been signed at Genoa, allowing the emigrants full rights—both to worship and to develop the land given to them in Paomia as they pleased. The only condition imposed on them was that the Pope should be recognised as the spiritual head of the Church and that in cases of necessity they should serve the Genoese Republic.

The Greeks were more than willing to accept the conditions and they at once constructed a town, built their own church, and began to cultivate the hills all round. The experiment looked as though it would be a success.

But when the Corsicans began their series of revolts against the Genoese, the Greeks, bound in allegiance to Genoa, were heavily persecuted. Eventually they were forced to give up their settlements in Paomia and go to Ajaccio—abandoning their possessions, and their vineyards, unable, for fear of being recognised, to wear their national costume. It was only when the French took over the government that the Greeks were able to return; to a place slightly west of the old site, where Cargésé now stands.

Relations, never very friendly with the surrounding villages—who were continually resentful of the Greeks, allying them mentally with the Genoese—deteriorated again during the Revolution and a second time Cargésé had to be abandoned. The Greeks returned to Ajaccio leaving behind them a burning city.

In 1814 they went back for the final time and restarted life in the ruins of the old town. Gradually the native barriers were broken down, intermarriage began, and the Corsican dialect superseded Greek as the common language.

Now hardly more than three families still speak Greek. The Orthodox Church still remains, but little else—a few names, some straight Greek noses, a sense of comparative order, and the pure olive skins and dark eyes in occasional faces.

. . . . .

Towards evening the heat died away. The sea became glassy as though scraped clean of waves by the blade of a knife. Noises grew clearer—a child's voice crying as it swung in a hammock, a man arguing, the anguished bray of a donkey.

Placidity hung everywhere, something different from the sapped listlessness of the day, the irritable ennui of the heat. It made the landscape, the houses washed with sunset, the people, and the dry plants all of one piece—with time on the hands and sufficient to do in the simple act of existence.

The smoke-coloured air merged into the headland, and a mist drew itself over the sea in a screen. Lights came out, faded, tinselly stars, like the painted canopy on the blue roof of the Greek church.

The sound of silver clattered under the trellised grapes in the garden. A goat shook its bell on the hill of olives. Time went on somewhere else, under a different sky.

. . . . .

After dinner a young man came down from Evisa—thirty miles or so inland in the mountains. His father was an officer in the French Zone of Germany—he, too, was blond and very German-looking,

144

CARGÉSÉ

speaking German with a conscious superiority over the peasants listening outside the Café des Amis.

The young man spoke with contempt of the fishermen, of the people round the coasts—"The real Corsicans are in the mountains," he said, "not amongst this malaria and laziness. These people are no good"— the German accent floated arrogantly over the fine, uncomprehending faces, "up in the hills we all carry pistols."

The pistol was the last symbol of the Vendetta, the romantic link with the past, with Sampiero, Romanetti and Paoli. Blood must revenge blood, even though now there was little to revenge.

The *boches*, the *lucquois* had gone. But Corsica had been the first country to be liberated, the *montagnards* had been the real *maquis*— to which they had given their name—the bren guns landed in hidden bays by submarine had given a new life to the romantic symbol.

The self-dramatizations, the arrogance trembled in the boy's voice. "Everyone in the mountains has pistols," he repeated. "These people are no good."

.   .   .   .   .

There was no hotel open in Cargésé, but a nice restaurant with tables in a garden looking onto the sea. A few streets away there was a room in a *pension*, inevitably shuttered up from the sun and full of the usual Second Empire *bric-a-brac*, but clean, and, when the shutters were open, with a view over the two churches and the hillside dropping away into the Gulf of Sagone.

The town had very little life of its own—two or three cafés nearly always empty, about four shops, and the beach. During the day it seemed practically derelict—half the houses were boarded up and no one walked about except the few washerwomen and the fishermen below. But there were not more than a dozen even of them.

At night, instead of the usual dance music raucously churned out of café gramophones, the silence merely deepened. People sat on benches in the shadows, talking in quiet voices. Dim lamps glowed like small fires in tenement windows, with the moon shining on the sea at the back of the narrow streets.

Life had passed its climax; a long time ago something had happened, and now it was all over. It was no longer interesting to discuss.

Instead the moon came over the Rue Marbœuf lighting up the hidden faces like a passing camera. Below, the palm trees spread out stiff, arrested arms through which the chromium sea slowly poured itself backwards and forwards. And all through the night the flies lay over

146

CARGÉSE

the bedroom walls like currants; a child coughed downstairs, pitifully and with effort; the heat broke up against the bedrails, wet and uncertain.

In the morning the blue sky came in cloudlessly, and the smell of refuse from the lavatory patch piled up outside the open windows.

INSTEAD OF A LITERATURE

Corsican literature, as such, does not exist. All the art and poetry which Corsica possesses goes into the oral songs and laments which are sung on special occasions—the *vocero* which is sung in front of a dead man killed in vendetta, the *serenata* which is the love song, the *lamento* which is the mourning of natural death, and the *ballata*—sung to describe the exploits of famous or legendary men.

The *vocero*, particularly, is dramatic in character—a rehearsal by the dead man's relatives of the revenge which they are bound to undertake. It is more than an expression of grief, much more than natural emotion. For fundamentally the *vocero* is a call to war, a whipping-up of the urge for vengeance which is to be the dominating factor of their future lives.

The singing is usually begun by the closest relative—the wife or mother of the deceased. At first it is tender, full of loving phrases and nicknames, " *O mon cerf au poil brun* ", " *Mon faucon sans ailes* ". Then the grief is slowly wrought up to a crisis, with dancing round the body, hands touching the wounds, and short, sharp cries, like the cries of sexual love, leading up to hysterical orgasms of grief, with tears, masochism, passion and hatred mixed up together.

The songs all follow the same theme, improvised round the words of the famous " *O Matté di la Surella* ", which celebrated the death of Giovanni Matteo, killed by Ricciottu and Mascarone, and which was sung by his sister:

> *O Matteo, frère chéri,*
> *De ton sang précieux,*
> *Ils en ont lavé la place,*
> *Ils en ont baigné l'enclos,*
> *Il n'est plus temps de dormir,*
> *Il n'est plus temps de se reposer.*
>
> *Que tardes-tu, O Cecc'Anto ?*
> *Extirpe tripes et boyaux*
> *De Ricciottu et Mascarone,*

Jette-les en pâture aux oiseaux,
Oh! qu'une nuée de corbeaux
Leur devorent les chairs et mettent les os nus.

Oh! Dominique mon cousin
Arme-toi et fais un exemple terrifiant,
Ils se sont vantés sur la place,
Ils ont dit que tu étais vieux,
Et qu' aux menaces des femmes,
Ils ne prêtaient pas d'oreilles.

Si j'avais un garçon,
Je lui taillerais un gilet
Dans mon tablier ensanglanté,
Afin qu'il n'oublié jamais
Le sang de mon frère,
Et que, devenu grand,
Il fasse le massacre.

Comme mon coeur est noir
Je veux noircir mes vêtements
Qui, O Jean-Mathieu,
Va me dédommager de ta perte?
Qui va expier mes peines?
Mes larmes . . . mes tourments?

Like all classical drama, it is woven round obligation—in this case the necessity of answering blood with blood. Civil law, religious teaching, reason—these are all thrown to the winds in the sublime urgency of family honour. It is something beyond the scope of Christian ethics,

> "*Plutôt que de ne pas voir sa vendetta,*
> *Je renoncerai à mon baptême.*"

something which cannot risk the hazard of impartial justice.

But with the establishment of social order by the French, and the more or less complete elimination of the *vendetta* except in the mountains, the wilder aspects of the *vocero* have disappeared. Instead there are the wonderfully poignant *lamenti*, with their intimate lover's similes of loss, "*Vous étiez a mes yeux une voile à la mer*" and their flowering blessings, "*Puisse-t-il de ta belle chair immaculée éclore des violettes.*" "*Des fleurs sur cette fleur.*"

150

Nearly all Corsican songs, even the *serenata*, are sad—preoccupied with the evanescence of life or love, the fatalism of suffering running through them. The expression of gaiety, or of pure joy is something quite alien—the moment of love or happiness is itself tinged with regret, for as soon as it is experienced it is already over.

These songs are all in the Corsican dialect—something nearer to Italian than to French, with its sing-song repetitive rhythms and its undertone of complaint. But the written literature about Corsica is all in French—and by French writers.

It seemed in a way surprising that no resentment born of natural historical causes should have existed against French domination—that not even a minority movement for independence should have arisen with the general movement for re-awakened national causes. But the French assimilation is complete and appears final. "*La Sampiera*", the war song of the Corsican National Front, has this refrain :

> "*Debout Corses! Corses debout!*
> *Soyez Corses et Français!*"

In the nineteenth century there was a sudden romantic interest in Corsica, and nearly all the works of any literary value which exist were written then. Merimée's *Colomba* (1839) was the first Corsican classic—the first book that treated the Corsicans with a certain realistic understanding, in contrast to the sort of flamboyant theatricalism of Dumas' *Les Frères Corses*, and the novelettish romanticism which succeeded it.

Subsequently both Daudet and Maupassant visited Corsica and laid the scenes of various stories there—Daudet's *Etudes et Paysages, Lettres de Mon Moulin* and *Rose et Ninette*; Maupassant's *Contes*— with descriptions of Ajaccio and the monastery at Corbara—and *Une Vie*.

In 1840 Flaubert published a journal of a short tour—*Voyage en Corse*—enthusiastic and slightly naïve notes written when he was very young, with some beautifully fresh descriptive pieces, full of romantic nostalgia.

Albert Glatigny, travelling round the island a few years after Flaubert, wrote his best prose work—*Le Jour de l'An d'un Vagabond*—after having been imprisoned in Ajaccio in mistake for a well-known bandit. But his book is a simple acclamation of landscape beauty, with a Rousseauesque reaction to Nature—elemental, full of sentiment and wonder.

In all these books—as well as in works like Bergerat's *La Chasse au Mouflon*—the emphasis is on landscape and on peasant traditions, with the exception of a few of Daudet's stories that deal with minor intrigues in Ajaccio. But they deal with a life that in its own way was alive.

Since then the seedy commercialism of a more accessible continent has changed the atmosphere in which the people live—the landscape remains the same, but the towns are all infected with the lethargic decay which is common to all places where the centre of life has moved away.

So Corsican literature has ceased to be a reality. Like the nineteenth century writers who created it, its interest has gone back to France, its literary regionalism dissolved in a larger unity.

A DREAM

DURING the night the insects grew huge. The flies stared down from enormous eyes, sharpening antennae the size of scythes. Moving in an under-water light, snakes wriggled up onto the beach, nesting in the thighs; lizards like alligators circled round in the darkness, only their eyes glistening under their elephantine lids.

Through a jungle of swamp, an army of overgrown spiders lurched on stilts closer and closer, crowding in till there was nowhere else in the world to go—and every place in the mind's eye map swarmed suddenly with reptiles, repeating ,"Not here ! Not here !"

PORTRAITS IN A BUS

IN A bus one learns everything. There was, for instance, the Communist, a pale, faded flower of a man with distinction drained into weakness, who came from Vico and was going back to work in Marseilles.

He had expressive, thin hands which he waved to describe the iniquities of capitalism—throwing out the fingers like antennae to express his points. Over and over again the same parallel, De Gaulle and Churchill. But he was a peasant by birth, with the romantic camaraderie of the soil, so he understood equality better than power.

He had gone to school in Marseilles and married a Parisienne. His good looks had lifted him into a different world, a world more suited to his appearance. He knew all the right names—Baudelaire, Dante, Shakespeare, Racine—and mentioning each he stopped as if mesmerised by the sound of the words or of some intimate vision they conjured up. But he liked most of all La Fontaine, reciting it there in the bus with the people in front edging round, the old peasants uncomfortably ignorant of what was going on, the young girls fingering their crucifixes and giggling.

Then the middle-aged couple from Lyons—he, good-looking but running to fat in a particularly French sort of way, she, auburn-haired and acquiescive, but both of them obsessed with the idea of malaria. "Have you taken your quinine? You must take it at least three times a day"—a sort of elementary French conversation lesson—"the doctor at Porto gives it out free, you know. You should get some at once, the mosquitoes are all riddled with fever," and she looking up at him, agreeing, as she must have done all through their married life.

Opposite, a French painter and his wife—civilised, and complaining of the bill in the Porto hotel, which was extortionate. With them was a magistrate on holiday who had refused to pay and when he threatened to report the price to the police, the hotel had said, "Very well, pay what you like"— On the coast the small inns and hotels were like that—grasping, dirty, with a sort of *petit bourgeois* bonhomie that quickly turned into calculation.

All round, peasant women—grey skinned, with black dresses enveloping the dirt with greasy folds and children staring out from

154

unwashed faces. An old man with a cloth cap, who had been one of the leaders of the underground—"At night the submarines used to put into the inlet where I live, and as mine was the only house, I used to take off the supplies and the guns, and next night take them up into the mountain. *Beaucoup des Anglais*," he said, knocking out his pipe on the window ledge and collecting the spittle up in his throat.

But most of the faces might be from anywhere—men in their shirt-sleeves, with fair receding hair and the air of clerks; young girls with coloured, print frocks and sallow complexions, looking out of the window without any expression whatever—they might have been waitresses in an ABC Cafeteria; white-haired housewives in spectacles, buxom and with heavily veined faces like the women in the public bars of Camden Town. Nothing distinctive, nothing to mark them down as people of one time and place. The bus might have been going over the edge of the world, but there would have been no more animation, no more comprehension.

.　　.　　.　　.　　.

Near Ajaccio, an aeroplane came out of the sun and slowly taxied over the airfield. Civilisation returned through a series of symbols— an advertisement for the Hotel Napoléon Buonaparte, scrawled chalk signs "*Votez pour Francini*", warehouses humped together at the end of jetties with small coaling ships dirtying the air.

Then down by the sea the wonderful wide sweep of the harbour unfolded itself, the white fan of the town with combs of palm trees sticking up, and the papery sailing boats leaning against the heat. Up past the station, the cafés had their chairs already out and water showered over the stone pavements; melons lay in the gutter and in the main streets the smart negresses stalked about in white shorts, the smell of bougainvillaea coming over from the Préfeture garden and the French flag hanging limply over dark shrubs.

In the Place de Gaulle the passengers off the Tunis boat sat about outside the Hotel de France; the café politicians in white drill leaned back from their morning papers and the newsboys cried out amongst the polished tables "*Manolete est mort, Manolete, le toréador, est mort!*" From the harbour the smoke from the ships uncurled against the mountains into a pale turquoise sky.

STUDIES ON A BEACH

THE SUN shines all Sunday. Girls lie about on the rocks at Ariadne like exotic flowers washed up by the tide —red and green ribs of colour over bodies spreadeagled with sun.

The sea fondles about at their feet, their hands move flicking off flies, the secret consummation with the sun goes on uninterrupted.

The water is displaced as three enormous figures advance out of the afternoon. Three horizontally striped costumes, woollen and loose, draping a *boulanger*, his wife and sister. The soft, man's stomach, fleshily white, floats above the water, a partially uncovered island. Then the two women, varicose-veined, shrieking, waddle over two feet of sea. Like three liners cavorting in love play, they splash one another, throw water down the alleys of their breasts, and retire into shadows to sleep.

The draped flowers cross their legs over the sun. Then later the supercilious young men in red and white flowered trunks walk at the water's edge, throwing a ball about in the air. A speedboat dallies off shore, circling round the bathers like a temptation. But there is nothing worth catching, so it slews round and makes out to sea where a solitary fishing boat is marooned off the Sanguinares.

At sunset the *Portugal* comes steaming out of the bay, a Queen Mother among the small harbour craft that chug about on odd jobs. The noise of her siren, conjuring up all the uncapturable emotions that never really existed, shatters the evening's complacency.

The flowers sit up, becoming girls, pick up handbags and go off amongst the olive trees to find drinks.

The shadows of the trees lengthen over the water and the band strikes up at Marinella. Cicadas crowd in over the bougainvillaea and cactus.

LE ROI JÉROME

AFTER dinner the fashionable thing to do was to go and drink coffee in the Roi Jérome. Between nine and ten every evening all the beach girls, the black marketeers, the near-gangsters and a few others came in and sat about on plush chairs in a back room, while a bored young man in a canary pullover played very good jazz, a cigarette dropping ash up and down the keys, as he looked about the room through the gauze of cigarette smoke. It was the nearest approach in Corsica to the world of the American film—conscientiously but rather badly aped.

All round the room the girls draped themselves, showing ribbons of brown thigh, and pecking genteelly at their coffee cups. But the remarkable thing was that hardly anyone drank alcohol—in about an hour and a half, with about thirty people constantly there, the waiter said he served only three liqueurs and two Cinzanos. For the rest, people drank coffee, brightly coloured *sirops*—with frightful watered down flavours of peppermint or raspberry—and, of course, *pastis*. Throughout Corsica, in fact, apart from the ordinary wine they drank in their own houses, the people seemed to drink very little. Only on Saints' Days, by some curious connection of religion with intoxication, was there any evidence of alcohol being drunk with the idea of stimulus or excitement.

But the pianist never for a moment stopped playing, languid, sentimental American tunes, all slightly hotted-up, and the dark, greasy-haired men in two-coloured striped jerseys lounged about on the chairs smoking or playing bélote, and paying very little attention to the music or the girls. Bits of paper were brought out with figures on them, hands waved pointing out this and that—all the various bits of black market fiddling which together produced a reasonable income spent in Marseilles or Tunis, but never in Corsica.

In the outer room, at a chromium bar stuck up with pictures of French film stars, a pallid middle-aged woman, blonde hair streaked with white done up in a bun, sat swinging grotesquely naked legs— the nakedness accentuated by the unsunburnt, flabby flesh—and smoked in long, slow puffs from an enamel cigarette-holder.

Nobody took any notice of her, but the fantastic, exaggerated performance went on as if a thousand eyes were fixed on every gesture. She

wore royal blue trousers, just too long for shorts and a shade too short for the contemporarily smart three-quarter lengths. Nightly, the barman said, she came in and sat there, one hand on hip, a simulated glazed look surveying the room through half-shut eyelids, and the smoke uncurling up against the pink and blue frieze of streamlined girls that stretched round the walls. But never, he said, with any result. By the bar the proprietor, a fat, completely bald little man with a face like Sidney Greenstreet, meticulously jotted down each coffee and each *sirop* in columns on a huge sheet of paper stretched out on a table.

"You like guitars?" he said, "this music is no good," and he made a contemptuous gesture towards the inner room where boogie-woogie was drumming out, "but the customers like it. You are English, yes?" he went on, "I was once imprisoned by the Italians as an English spy." He burst into a deep, throaty gurgle, his face squeezing up like a baby's. "During the war the English come by night," he made repeated parachute gestures, gurgling away happily with all the coffee ticking forgotten, "and I help them with food. The Italians ask me if I'm French and I say No! Corsican"—that was his favourite remark, for he had a loathing for the French and a complete belief in the individuality of his own nationality, which was almost unique—"but they took me off to the camp with the English. Ah! the *lucquois*," he made savage

158

contemptuous gestures, grotesque on his crumpled up child's face, "they are no use. In a few days I was back up here." He laughed, clapping his thigh with his podgy little hands, then suddenly became serious. "But I will take you to the guitars, only a little café for the people, you know, but the music is beautiful, you will see." He ticked off two more coffees laboriously, then threw away the pencil. "Come," he said, "I will show you the real Corsica, not like this place," and he screwed up his face like a schoolboy taking castor oil.

He led the way down a few backstreets to where a chink of light lit up a small interior of a bar, with three or four tables out in front of it and a girl and two men playing cards inside. Sitting round the entrance a few figures moved behind the glowing ends of their cigarettes in the darkness.

But King Jérome, as they called him, was well known, for as soon as they caught sight of him, they all got up guiltily from the pavement and went inside. By the time he had ordered cherry brandies, two of them had drawn up chairs and were tuning up on their guitars—good-natured,

fine-eyed boys who smiled at him while they played as though they were humouring a peculiarly childish whim.

When they began playing he sat with his head between his hands, the light shining on the huge, salmon-coloured dome, and gazed at the guitar with a look of drugged ecstasy—the far-away absorption that mediums put on in a trance. Then a boy began to sing. The music began with the harsh plaintive, almost epileptic choke in the throat that is common to so much oriental chanting—very sad, with an overtone of hysteria about it, then falling away into a tender, soft lament. The boy who sang was exquisitely beautiful, but very self-conscious, laughing all the time as if it all was really rather absurd and suddenly breaking into tangos which made King Jérome very petulant. "*Pas Espagnol, pas Americain, pas Français, mais Corse!*" he kept bursting out, his reverie abruptly shattered. "If you don't sing properly, in Corsican," he said, "I'm going back to my bar."

So they started off again, solemnly serious, a few bars of some grief-laden love song, while the little fat figure rearranged itself into its position of surrender and drank in the delicate, sweet tones of the serenade. The boy's voice rose and fell, expressive and gentle, while the dark eyes behind smiled all the time as though telling a nursery rhyme and then suddenly, with the spell at its height and the slopped figure entranced, the guitars broke into ragtime again, unconsciously almost, and the boy started laughing. The little man got up and banged the table with his fists, hopelessly. Then, giving the boy up as a bad job, he called out to the girl who was playing cards. "Will you sing a little, Madame?" he said. "I have some friends." The girl was very pretty and smiled obligingly in a mechanical way. She was the wife of the proprietor of the café—it was called Au Son des Guitares Bar—who was one of the young men playing the guitars, indolent and pleasantly fleshy. "Certainly," she said, "what would you like?"

"Anything," he said, "but in Corsican, please, please." The little voice wailed out to her imploringly, the hands stretched out as if registering emotion in a silent film.

She began to sing; a hard, strident voice which she projected straight in front of her down some imaginary microphone, at the same time going on with the game of cards. It was the same sort of tune as before, a mixture of grief and love, rising to sudden moments of frenzy—but she sang it completely without expression, so that in its indifferent hardness it acquired a particular, brittle sexuality—as though all the time love was being made to her under the table but she was purposely taking no notice.

At the end of the song the fat, doll's figure got up and thanked her, beaming through his glasses, satisfied that something had been completed at last. He was all hardness and ruthlessness except in these two things—being a Corsican and wallowing in the sentiment of the national music, and on the subject of having helped the English during the war. Everything, it became obvious, could be got from him by indulging him in talking about the war and in playing Corsican music.

Once it was finished he became at once the business man again. "I must go back to business," he said with distaste outside, and already the thump of the piano in the Roi Jérome could be heard coming over the dark streets, with its atmosphere of plush chairs, of smoke wreathing up round the pastel wallpaper and bored girls lying about with bare stomachs and thighs.

He screwed up his face again and spat, "What filthy music ! All the fault of the Americans," he said, then burst into his guttural chuckle. "But six or seven of them were shot here every night. Bang ! Bang !" He stopped in the street and laughed, as if the memory of it was too much for him.

"Oh ! yes," he went on, "they think they buy everything, but bang ! bang ! they buy that too," and he bent up double laughing. "They are worse than the French," he said, "much worse."

161

MARINELLA

ABOUT ten-thirty every night the people emptied out of the Jérome and piled into the buses waiting in the Place de Gaulle. From then till one in the morning, overloaded buses left at half-hourly intervals for the beaches.

Moving along the shadow of the mountains, with the moon coming like glass off the sea and the palm trees disappearing into the water at the end of the Scudo headland, the incongruousness of the whole amosphere increased its air of unreality. It became impossible to believe in the juxtaposition of such opposed ways of life within such short distances. From east to west the island is only about fifty miles, yet five miles from the sea on all the coasts life has ended. The mountains which form the whole island, except for narrow strips at the sea's edge, create a series of frontiers as absolute as if there were hundreds of miles in between. So each community is shut off from the others, with only very tenuous links joining them all to Ajaccio. There is no direct communication between any of the towns—everything has to go through the centres of Ajaccio, Bastia or Corte. From there life is re-distributed. But in the normal course of events, families living in the villages and smaller towns have never visited places ten miles away because there is no direct route. Each of them knows its own village and Ajaccio or Bastia. Behind the mountains another continent with another civilisation might exist—but to the people living all round it is only a few lights in the night, a fabulous, legendary city which is no more real than a mirage.

But coming round the bend of Barbacaja, with the wind blowing through the sloping, open windscreens of the bus, the lights of Marinella seemed very real. Hidden in the darkness, with the black tents of hills pointing up like robed figures behind, and in front the sea rippling with soft chromium, two squares of neon lights hung up in the air.

A small alcove of light, with dim figures moving against the bulbs, stretched out into an illumined diving board that made a circuit into the sea and then came back to land again. A raised wooden platform held half a dozen tables with a cocktail bar and a three-piece orchestra at the far end. All round on the sand people sat at tables with the seas lapping right up to their feet.

There were two of these oases of light in about five hundred yards

162

of beach. At the far one there were many more tables and much more light—by the time the bus had unloaded, the tables were all full, so couples sat about on the sand with the cactus making grotesque caricatures over their heads.

On the postage-stamp of dancing floor about twenty couples tangoed to the South American music, which was ceaselessly played all night. Nearly every couple was negro, or mixed in colour—negresses in print frocks and bell skirts dancing with middle-aged Corsicans, negro sailors with blondes held up tight in a drug of passion, and then pure negro couples, slowly revolving in some long drawn-out ritual that fell away weakly when the music stopped. But only for a few minutes, because there were scarcely any pauses as no one ever drank anything except the tourists, and the same half-filled glasses of brightly coloured water stood on the tables the whole time.

The second place, the Palm Beach, had a much better band but was far less crowded and hardly anyone danced. There were no negroes there at all, but odd groups of people sitting about talking, a solitary blonde dance hostess who didn't get asked to dance all evening, and tables with four or five boys or girls sitting together—never mixed. Occasionally the boys came over and took the girls off to dance, but when the music stopped they simply turned away and went back to their own groups without saying a word. It was impossible to tell what really went on between them—whether really there was nothing to say or whether it was all said in private at some other time and no residue was left.

The whole thing was superbly beautiful—the harbour lights of Ajaccio just visible, the voices murmuring in the semi-darkness, the music being carried away over the wash of sea, with the perfume of the *maquis* unrolling itself from the dark hillsides—but still it was without animation. Somewhere else always the real life seemed to be going on, secretly and out of sight.

After midnight the tables began to thin out and people began walking back along the beaches—momentarily lit up as the stream of buses came flying from Marinella, the drivers swinging recklessly round bends as if suddenly a time-table had to be made up. Bus drivers in fact were the really only vital people in Corsica—reckless heroes, like early flyers, who navigated the mountains and coast roads with a complete disregard of caution and with uncanny skill.

But the music went on well into the dawn, with the negroes indefatigably revolving in hypnotic circles and the band playing the same tangos over and over again.

163

Back in the town, past the enormous, tiled cemetery, nothing moved in the empty square, and only the lingering smell of damp fireworks clustered like stale sweets round the plane trees.

THE NAPOLEON TOUR

THE AGENCY officials had said that a
bus for the airfield would run from the Rue Buonaparte at nine in the
morning. The plane was due to leave at ten o'clock and arrive in
Marseilles at eleven-thirty.

Needless to say, it did not. There had been a violent storm in the
night which had left the sky cloudy and a slight breeze had kicked up
the sea into a few white horses. From early on, the flying boats and
Air France planes could be seen taking off and coming in, but it was
apparently too much for the Alpes-Provence pilots.

"Come back at one o'clock," they said in the office, "the weather is
a little rough," and the man at the desk pointed to the wisp of grey
cloud streaming very quickly below the great blue canvas that stretched
away behind. The time-table became of no consequence; it was as if
some act of God had rendered all competition with the elements, however slight they were, absolutely impossible. "Later," he said, and went
back to the paper spread out on the desk.

Actually it was not a bad thing, for it left us unexpected time to see
the guide-book sights, which in the hot sun had seemed far too unappetis-
ing to make the effort worth while. But now with an extra morning to
fill in, no sun and the only pleasant breeze that had blown in our whole
visit, a fresh interest in the respectable relics of history re-asserted itself.

First of all, of course, there was the house where Napoleon was
born. You came to it, after passing along the Rue Danielle Casanova
—named after the young Communist leader who had been tortured
to death in Auschwitz—where there was a small plaque on the house of
her birth commemorating her achievements for France and encouraging
the youth of her country to follow her example on the way towards
"*les lendemains qui chantent*".

Then along by the sea wall, with the breakers lapping up over the
rocks, past the house built by Napoleon III and the Empress Eugénie,
till you reached a small street turning up almost shamefacedly into a
semi-slum. In the middle of crossed cobbled streets, with children
playing about amongst refuse and gutters filled with discarded fruit,
candles burned on the altar of a church with a faded green campanile
raising itself over the tenement roofs.

At right angles to the church ran the Rue St. Charles, where, three-quarters of the way down, a little tablet on a house wall marked the birthplace of Napoleon the First, Emperor of the French.

The cost of entry was sixteen francs. A pleasant-faced, stoutish woman, middle-aged and in an apron, came to the door and started off at once on a conducted tour with brief dissertations on all the rooms.

Inside, the house was much larger than its rather unprepossessing exterior and surroundings suggested. Living rooms, sparsely filled with period furniture, opened out on either side of the door and shutters flung open let the light in on simple but good-sized morning rooms. Then up a flight of stairs a long reception room with four windows on either side and delicately carved chairs all along the walls led to the wing where Napoleon had his own rooms.

The caretaker pointed out the small, low divan on which he was born, the bedroom he always used, the study and dining-room he shared with his mother—all of them a little dusty but respectable, with a faded elegance and spaciousness that presumed a way of life above the average of the mean little streets that spread their dirt beneath the tall windows.

In an emptied salon a table stood by the door, with postcards laid out all over it—views of the house from the small garden opposite, a picture of Laetitia's bed, a romanticised portrait of Napoleon on the Pont d'Arcole, and little miniatures of the Imperial family all grouped together on one card, the whole fourteen of them, Napoleon in the centre with a crown of oak leaves, the Empresses Marie Louise and Josephine in ornate head-dresses, the Princesses with Queen Caroline and Queen Hortense gazing insipidly across at their brothers—Lucien, Jérome, Joseph, Louis all in different and extravagant costumes.

But the feeling that something had taken place here once was more real than in most places. The remains of a certain introspective grandeur showed through under the dust and the bareness of the rooms seemed to increase one's awareness that a central figure was missing—a presence that had made itself felt and which now left a gap that the dutiful reverence of tourists could never quite bridge.

Outside the sky was still grey and the wind if anything had increased. Someone had scrawled, ironically enough, in large chalk letters on the wall facing Napoleon's house, "*Vive de Gaulle et Vive l'Angleterre.*"

The road at the bottom led up towards the Cours Grandval at the top of which, in a ledge on the hillside, the real Napoleonic statue looked down over the town onto the harbour. Halfway up the road, beyond a levelled out square with trees planted all round it, the statue came in sight—a grey green figure with cocked hat and hand inside the

166

coat, at the top of magnificent, sloping-back marble steps inlaid with lettering.

As memorials go it was superb in its way—high up and away from the town, the face curiously young and plump-looking, like a business man's grown successful too early—and the figure framed with a mound of olive trees interspersed with flowers. The sun came out for a few seconds, so the white of the base stood out dazzling and impossible to look at, while the great letters carved out their dates and facts under the confident, lonely statue.

Nothing passed by near it and it was not visible from any of the roads that were ordinarily used—it was at the back of everything, an unseen power who gave silent audience only to those who made the deliberate pilgrimage up the hill, as if inside the stone the Imperial spirit was still sealed up, breathing out its vain orders.

RETURN FLIGHT

THE MORNING was very fine, with a deepening blue sky, and sun-light lying across all the harbour buildings touching them into life like a sword. But the heat was finished—already the air had its first undertones of autumn and the sun seemed washed out of its fever.

The drive up to the airfield showed the leaves lined up under the plane trees at the side of the road. The chestnuts were foaming out in clusters of orange that protruded like dusters from the sugary buildings as the road climbed up over the town, and the whole port shimmered in a slight haze.

Through the olive groves the wings of the plane could be seen shivering as the motors revved up, with the pilot and mechanic already waiting on the runway.

In five minutes the plane was in the air—the frontier was passed at the edge of the cliff, with the prisoners working on the aerodrome glued to the ground, growing smaller and smaller.

One grows accustomed to being in a place, feeling secure there, as though only a great effort of will would ever get one off——yet when it actually happens, it is all done nonchalantly, painlessly, with no sense of achievement at all.

The peasants looking out of the tiny windows, watching their past dropping away like a stone, and their expressionless faces gradually taking on new life—was there no wrench there, no brittle severing of the nerves that appeared to bind them so surely ?

The white buildings of Ajaccio fell out of sight like staring faces; the sea began to flow past the panel of window in faint crêpe ripples.

After an hour the French coast came into sight—only seventy-minutes flying time away, yet a different world had built itself up some where in the blue wastes of feeling.

Gradually it swayed into view—long thin jetties cradling model liners, yellow and impregnable looking castles clamped onto rocks, the red, dove-tailed roofs of buildings slowly spreading into warehouses and marshalling yards, with smudges of smoke fading away into the blank sky.

Then the great, white ribbon of the runway rose up from the bottom of the hills, with M-A-R-S-E-I-L-L-E-S spelt out in huge letters on the

green turf; and slowly, coming into land, the peasants looked with their heavy animal eyes at the concrete pressing up to meet them.

In the air station, with the sun shining cleanly through the polished glass windows, and the glossy magazines a riot of colour against the white distemper of the walls, the values of an old existence, like a currency, became valid again—but with God knows what hopes, what disillusions, what difficulties, while somewhere over the horizon people were sitting peacefully under palm trees, time going on without danger, with no more change than a man spitting against a crumbling building, the sunset streaking over the blue sea, an aeroplane coming into land. . . .

NAPOLEON BONAPA

A Framework of History

500 B.C. to 1077 A.D.	Greeks, Carthaginians, Romans, Vandals, Byzantines, Tuscans in turn occupy the island.
1077	Corsicans become subjects of Genoa.
1077 to 1568	Genoese Rule.
1688	Greek Immigration.
1735	General Assembly at Corte draws up Constitution of Corsican Independence.
1736	Landing of Theodor I.
1737	Genoese enlist French help to subdue the island. War commences against the French.
1751	French Rule.
1752	French expelled. War with Genoese under leadership of Gaffori.
1755	Pasquale Paoli declared sole leader.
1759	Genoese enlist French aid.
1767	Genoese sell sovereignty of Corsica to France for £2,000,000. War against French ensues.
1769	Corsicans subdued by French. Napoleon born.
1790	Corsica a "department" of France.
1792	Paoli revolts: British help enlisted. British land: commence war against French.
1794	Corsica proclaimed part of British Empire.
1795 to 1796	Corsicans revolt against British misrule. British leave. Final acceptance of French rule.

PASQUALE PAOLI

For Michael Swan

Disorder was defeat, he knew; and so, acclaimed
by birth a natural leader, he returned home
from Naples and became a law, named
all his people brothers who could come
and at his feet lay troubles like a tribute.

His fame was bound up with belief, his God
the country of his dreams, whose good
grew to a moral force and made a rough-shod
peasant like a hero—the real God he stood
at night and prayed to for his dreams.

"*Una superbia indicibile*"—his heart alone
was Government and judge, his trust
his own imagined jury and the stone,
philosophy had formed into a charm,
that fate or conscience could not harm.

But in the end he lost, though did not lose
the hope that Providence ordained a meaning
in his loss—and so set off with scanty crews,
three hundred followers in all from Porto Vecchio, leaning
at sunset from the rails of his last ship.

And so the final glimpse was beauty, loss—
the island rose and dropped into the wineshot sea.
The ships' heads turned to west, the course
for England, and a page of history
shimmered like a sun and closed on liberty.

Then later when he died, his death
in London crowned with vines and wreaths
that lay upon his tomb like stars,
his whole life seemed to grow in stature;
though, afar, in Rostino they mourned a son.

PASQUALE PAOLI

THEODOR VON NEUHOFF

For Leonard Rosoman

Birth was not enough; for love and wealth
he killed a friend and lost his taste
for both; his only money was his health.
So somehow the debt must be effaced,
the honour somewhere make amends
for what he thought were worth-while ends.
Paris began the crazy game, the Duchesse
of Orléans the leading counter—his friends
were Alberoni, Riperda, and Law; it seemed
at first the gamble had come off, the swindle more
or less a Full House of his wildest dreams.

But then a new hand blossomed like a flower,
desire became a face behind an island window.
If wealth, why not a crown? a sudden shadow
lingered on his dream, and fell in a shower
of coins whose meaning was not plain—
this time at Genoa he gambled with men's lives,
played money for his Queen, assured a stake
for all who backed his arms—men's wives
adored his robes, and for their husbands' sakes
he made them Ladies, and created Counts.
But he did not count the cost or prize
that finally eluded him and failed his lies.

Good in itself he did not scorn with power,
and now a King he issued laws and coins,
proclaimed his Court but did not lower
the hopes he held of foreign arms. But signs
were bad, the Kingdom lingered in the air
but could not hold. The King became a spare.
He sailed away to recoup money for his fines.
The luck had turned, but still against all odds,

THEODOR VON NEUHOFF

with Dutch and British ships he stumbled back
to find the hand played out, his ships mere wads
of fodder with no foe. His Kingdom fell through lack
of interest. The dream had broken in his hand—
Fate dealt him Death, a pauper in a foreign land.

For Keith
Vaughan

RAMPARTS AT BONIFACIO

Through Time's wrong telescope, Sardinia
a backcloth for ships, dreams burning in fires;
the Spanish sea vibrates in green sighs.
Weighted, the sky breathes down dead desires;
through slit windows stare dead eyes.

Now the wind rattles doors in the towers,
desertion growing out of space like a hazard.
Cold dreams decay in the cemetery's stone flowers,
and what spring of life dried up in the fingers
whose scrawled words move over walls like lizards?

BOSWELL ON TOUR

For Ruth Sheradski and William Sansom

Armed with letters, he arrived, an Army—
the island, his terrain, was food for knowledge,
its people Characters, its noble General, God;
they thought him very eminent or balmy
—instead he balanced somewhere near the edge.

The scenery was nice, like murals, but no more,
a setting for an opera, or a landscape
suitable for love—and, as it happened, war.
The fight went to his head like wine,
the brand of liberty was his own design.

He found himself a hero, wrote his speeches
every day in notebooks, and preserved an awe
about him like a prophet—the best leeches
tended him when sick; he reached the shore.
They thought him all the while a secret envoy.

But everything he found, he could employ
later in books, in epigrams at after-dinner talks,
or earnestly let loose at Johnson on their walks.
As well he studied causes, histories, facts;
conscientiously he unearthed motives from their acts.

He got his views from all the best-briefed sources—
talked art with Paoli, the army with Marbœuf;
he even studied cattle and the local horses,
made notes on *moufflon*. There remained one thorn
—the Emperor Buonaparte was not yet born.

BOSWELL

LEAR IN CORSICA

For Julian and Kathleen Symons

He took a rubber bath, his Suliot, and his gifts;
found friends and beauty but could not find romance
except in books; he waited on the highway as for lifts
but saw no pistol pointed at his head;
regretful, though relieved, he wrote " Romance is dead ".

He packed his Nonsense up, like love, inside a box;
instead he courted Views, the ilex-groves, the sea,
but, always careful, stopped to change his socks
when caught in storms and could not quite get in—
he travelled in a coach, but had no sense of Sin.

For, fifty-six, his comfort had become a vice,
his work dependent on his sleep and board;
and all the while he kept his verse on ice,
wrote prose, a little drab, to pass the time;
but was always happiest with a secret rhyme.

The island was a drink he drained of pleasure,
made daily drawings, sketches, journals, notes,
which later he developed and engraved at leisure
and filled a book with copious facts and charts.
But somehow drama evaded him in all his arts.

EDWARD LEAR

SAMPIERO

For Wolfgang von Einsiedel

He was, they said, the greatest of them all,
but not for battles won or sieges raised,
nor even for the glory of his final fall;
the qualities were other that they praised.

They lay somewhere between the eyes
and mouth, a softening of that steel
which broke his enemies like flies.
The freedom of his glance became a seal.

They knew as well his human crime
was born from qualities of Hate,
which after death appeared, with time,
as Love that blossomed out too late.

GUIDEBOOKS

For SHEILA MACPHEE

SOME THINGS can all be logged, like dates;
the points of interest on the route, the best
hotels, the famous heroes with their tragic fates,
the types of landscapes and the ruined towers.
But guidebooks cannot tell you all the rest.

The real life goes on somewhere else, away
from lidos on the beach or staged, romantic ruins;
the picture postcards have their coloured say
in harbours bright with boats and sailing churches.
But life escapes them, groping in the lurch.

They do not conjure up the smells or dirt,
the children's sores who idle near the bay;
nor say that here, beneath a bloodstained shirt,
a man's heart stopped through lack of human pity.
The personal details, like indecencies, are wrapped away.

They might admit, in tones of conversation,
that these fields rotted through a lack of work,
while back at home big business crucified the nation,
and people died in half-forgotten swamps or hills
through lack of means to fight the plague that killed.

But on the printed page the words are dead,
with no more meaning than the slogan scrawled
in chalk for sold-out leaders in the village halls.
The real life went dry inside a peasant's head
who died in war to write his name upon these walls.

CORSICAN DRUGS

For VERA SLOCOMBE

A FASHIONABLE vice, a cliché, and a golden key—
these already the shimmering needle, the utility
package white in the shade of the hand, have meant
but discarded as meanings; for now, instead
of being real, they exist as a barter, are dead
money with only a transfer life that, like paint,
comes off, its real coinage false but exchangeable
—a passport to escape with an anonymous label.

So you see them nightly in these wonderful harbours
change hands, small boxes exchanged at the bars
as if they were pills, but not to be used for ages—
their value increasing like wine, till somebody pages
an ultimate owner, who can afford to drown
this sick island in dreams and make it sound.
And watching, I envy them, who are able to frown
at the heat with no other ambitions, than sometimes
to live in a bubble and delay its coming to ground.

PORTO VECCHIO

For Laurie Lee.

The table carries a bottle, peaches, glasses;
through leaves of olive the sun burns
underwater patterns, anchors, molasses.
In blue silence a wind, Time passes.
A man is no longer what he earns.

The tents of salt are gashed red
with reflections of buoys, the wind
carrying a drug of pinewood and dead
cactus. The shadows are weighted with heads
like dark olives, and the windows are blind.

HILL DONKEYS

For PEGGY BAXTER

THE FLIES hang in haloes round their heads,
or else deliberately walk across the muzzle
of their faces, contemptuous of the idle
flick they shiver out beneath their bridle
—for even when they work or softly nuzzle
into reeds, they're less important than the dead.

Indeed, they seem no more than patient
slaves, ordinary beasts whose overloaded backs
are used to suffering, but which never crack
through strain or knowledge of a hidden bent.
Only their nervous, immensely elegant feet
give them away—and picking their delicate
path through rocks, they betray their defeat.

CACTUS

For Alan Pryce-Jones

Like orators declaiming or the grotesque
rubbery silhouettes of boxers, the prickly
paws fondle and miss the blue husk
of the day, already grown hot and sickly.

Below where they puncture and point
on the smoking hills, the harbour rides
securely under prints of coral and scent,
as boats turn over the sun on their sides.

Only the cactus hints with its nervous
shadows that Time is, unnoticed, away
on its own—a guest without fuss
who has left a hole in the day

by his absence and a growing alarm
that somewhere, northward in Europe
away from the shade of indolent palms,
absurd orators, like cacti, strangle our hope.

ISLANDERS

For Jack Clark

THEY SIT sweating under green palms
the olive bay unravelled to their gaze,
while paper boats elude the arms
the mountains press in mauve embrace.

But now they never look beyond
the fringe of trees whose broad leaves flow
like dancers in the harbour wind—
beauty tired them long ago.

Instead, brought up to watch the hills
look down on them like governesses,
and know the sun's soft magnet fall
nightly amongst the forest's tresses,

they see it all in different terms
—how drought had spoilt the autumn grapes
and war destroyed the private dreams
they'd mapped out for their own escape.

For now they see themselves condemned
like prisoners by the dwarfing sea,
and all around their future hemmed
in by their own absorbing pity.

BIBLIOGRAPHY

For the various historically informative passages in the book, I am indebted to the following works:

An Account of Corsica—James Boswell, 1769
Journal of a Landscape Painter—Edward Lear, 1868.
Corsica the Beautiful—A. Dugmore Hardie.
Corbara—Comte Pierre Savelli de Guido.
L'Ame de la Corse (anthologie)—G. Roger.
Vers l'Ile Captive—Jean-Martin Franchi.